BODY TURN TO RAIN

New & Selected Poems

BODY TURN TO RAIN

New & Selected Poems

»»»»»» Richard Robbins »»»»»»

A Northwest Masters Series Book from

LynxHousePress
Spokane, Washington

Northwest Masters Series | Christopher Howell: Editor

FIRST EDITION

Cover Art by Brian Frink, "Constellation Setting," watercolor, 2016.
Book Design: Christine Holbert.

LYNX HOUSE PRESS books are distributed by the University of Washington Press, 4333 Brooklyn Avenue NE, Seattle, WA 98195-9570.

Library of Congress Cataloging-in-Publication Data is available from the Library of Congress.

ISBN 978-0-8992415-1-7

TABLE OF CONTENTS

NEW POEMS

3. *Body Turn to Rain*

THE INVISIBLE WEDDING «««« 1984

FAMOUS PERSONS WE HAVE KNOWN «««« 2000

THE UNTESTED HAND «««« 2008

RADIOACTIVE CITY «««« 2009

OTHER AMERICAS «««« 2010

NEW POEMS

1. Mountain Daylight Time

TURPENTINE

Sometime try forgetting the roar of melted glacier
falling over stone toward whispering
cities in the basin. Or a wad of paper flaring
in an ashtray. Or in the hearth, the woods,
the ash-level rushing to meet flame
beneath the tipi made of sticks, the wind's language
launched at heaven. Sometime try forgetting

the leg as it broke, quiet knuckle,
or the melon-thump that day a speeding
biker died into the curb. Or the silence
all around him, and home. Sometime
smell, sometime taste the last bite of fish and watch
how it leaves you each time
you swallow wine or breathe. What if her hand

on your hand, still warm and floating only half
its weight now all these years since the day—
what if that weight dissolved
fast as the taste of herbs on carrots, what if
the eye having called it to mind
had to send it away for good, her hand
banished to the place memory

never reaches again. His voice calls you
to the creek. Sage smell like turpentine
and high desert. Then the small tug from the world

under water. The reeling. The flashing
coming your way. Its dance across roils. Its breading
each side of itself on the sand. Sometime
try forgetting what you know.

NEVER

Let's not pretend you never enjoyed rosehips
quivering all afternoon in Canada wind.
Or the sight of old men rounding the point
in their boat, bounding over last chop

before the calm of the bay. You watched
at the cleaning table as they slit
asshole to gill and seagulls hovered,
lucky cousins after a lottery, barking

their affection, diving for fistfuls
of gut held to surface by small bladders
of air. And don't forget coming home
early mornings, down the long dirt road

from the highway, lights off, the camp quiet, two
still down at the fire near the water telling
their story, keeping an eye on their star.
You slept between lilacs, then folded your bag

in daylight. You wrote poems under the same
bushes, a little chair eased up to a little table
with a typewriter, writing poems about
the day this all would leave you, as if that

immunized against loss, as if
somewhere in the universe at the same moment
a planet stepped out of its orbit to avoid
a collision of stardust and fate. You made

your beautiful poems, as if to become part
of the larch just beginning to turn
in early August, the nutcracker
hopping branch to branch, the weakening sun,

the char and salmon finding and dodging
each other under water. As if you could
become beauty and make it portable,
as if the cost was never seeing it again.

OLD COUNTRY PORTRAITS

My lost sister used to try the trick
with the tablecloth, waiting until
the wine had been poured, the gravy boat filled,
before snapping the linen her way

smug as a matador, staring down
silver and crystal that would dare move,
paying no mind to the ancestor gloom
gliding across the wallpaper like clouds

of a disapproving front—no hutch
or bureau spared, no lost sister sure
the trick would work this time, all those she loved
in another room, nibbling saltines,

or in the kitchen plating the last
of the roast beef. How amazed they would be
to be called to the mahogany room
for supper, to find something missing,

something beautiful, finally, they could
never explain, the wine twittering
in its half-globes, candles aflutter, each
thing in its place, or so it seemed then,

even though their lives had changed for good.

He thanked the cracked skin of his knuckle, the one
he barely knew until its collision
with plaster. He thanked the terra cotta head
and painted plate. He will tell the truth about them.
He thanked the close air. He thanked the small room
where he could praise, for the window bright
from fallen snow, for the fountain yards away

that will come on, the first day of April,
no matter what. He thanked the grandfather
on the wall, the boy he used to be
who stood next to him. He thanked the old man's
office on the 5th floor, Los Angeles, hills
filling the downtown window. He thanked

the Chinese elm, the rhododendra. He thanked
the grandmother and mother, hibiscus
wallpaper in the lacquered kitchen, 1959,
canasta parties, samba parties, the peanut butter
and mayonnaise sandwiches, the blue hair
of older women, the way one would laugh
before her dentures slipped. He thanked

the father, driving loads of rocket fuel across
the Mojave. He thanked the boat on the coldest
lake that side of Canada, and the salmon,
and the salmon, and the salmon. He thanked
the Northern Lights. He thanked the air and his own pulse.
He thanked the nights he slept outside, the sunrise,
waking to waves and one crow constantly

complaining. He thanked the person dying from stroke
in the middle of beauty. He thanked the person
drowned in a squall, the sailboat on its side
like a game piece. He thanked the drunk in the nearest
town, the train wreck a hundred miles from there,
1000 people poisoned 1000 miles away.
The truth is, they ran right into the green

cloud. The truth is, at the very end they fell
into each other like sacks of flour. He thanked
the wild rose on its spindly branch, pine pitch
and sage. He thanked the despot, God's horrible
clown. He thanked the black spots of disease.
He thanked the cage of his reason.
Thank you, he would say to his wife. Thank you,

to children, their awful freedom
beyond him. Thank you, to those I have injured.
The truth is, you did not deserve
the broken bone, the threat.
Thank you, darkness, hanging to the underside
of clouds. Thank you, to doors
open and closed

in the corridor behind me. Thank you,
breath coming in the window. Thank you, snow,
and the face that watches all along, its small mouth
the O I will live inside even after
leaving. He thanked the men he would never meet.
They would take everything, even the horse
on the painted plate, away.

THE TRUTH IS,

you came to me on a short
boat from a far island. You
came down the hill out of larch,

along the creek we both drink
from. You rose out of the green
coil of fern, tip of the sand

dune blowing lines of itself
away. If you hadn't said
my name, I wouldn't have looked

at your face. If I hadn't
looked, I wouldn't have turned to
glass on your desert floor, moss

under your quiet violin,
trout over your shallows, vole
racing across ancient duff

ahead of the owl's widening
shadow. I wouldn't have known
the oar on the forest floor

points west, having turned as wood
will do, mimicking iron,
toward an empty boat, a sea.

You didn't mean it, I hope, the day you walked into the surf like the last shot of a film, upright through the first surges of foam, even as you advanced toward the middle of the ocean, through the first wave breaking through your chest, upright through the swells beyond the break line to the point you might either float neck-deep or try to walk—even if the air in your lungs, even if your natural buoyancy would not allow it—beneath each swell toward dimmer and dimmer light. A lifeguard found you out before you disappeared. Pulled you back to shore. You didn't complain.

Or the day we made bread in the summer kitchen, a version of heaven or belief, dry breeze across the countertop. Your floured hands fluttered in the room with other living things, each now rising above a lip of metal, a small horizon.

Or the winter afternoon crossing the high Idaho meadow on our skis.

Or our first garden with its dozen zucchini, its infinite hope.

Versions of heaven or belief.

You didn't mean, I hope, to disappear from a certain part of day, then part of every day, to some system orbiting ours, one that returned you singed or frozen and with a different kind of look.

I have begun to talk to you with this pen to draw the permanent line between us. A pencil will sometimes lie.

LEAVING THE CITY

All the talk that night turned round
at the halfway point from wound

to religion, detoured south
past the cab stand, past all doubt

idling for a fare, to mouths
outracing this steel, that stone,

afraid of their oxygen,
the clouds gone, the towers pouting.

CALCULATION

The anatomy of desire led to
the mathematics of doubt, and that—
over months and months walking alone

through an iris garden drunk on its own perfume—
that led usually to the calculus
of grief or, in better days, those brief spells

between each drizzling front in off the coast,
in better days it led to the biometrics
of tenderness, the economy of lip and eyelash,

the sun coming through the window in sheets
onto the tousled sheets of the bed,
every limb akimbo as in an Escher print

where one leg of the body, pencil-gray but alive,
walks into the leg of the other, where one hand
draws the hand that draws itself. So much calculation

along the journey to affection, the emphatic
ear lobe and clavicle, the opera
of skin riding softly over each rib,

the Giacometti of a neck, the little hairs there,
the way only one side of mouth
smiles at the other's voice, two sides less often,

the way the heat of them passes back and forth
in the machinery of sex, the machinery
of loneliness a kind of whisper sent out,

called back before it reaches the ocean
of another ear. So much calculation
even after it ends: Crows paint

matrices on the sky, placing their Xs
there and there in an assembling,
dissolving theorem, their loud fermatas

claiming not certainty, not doubt, not non-belief
but a reckoning of wonder, high up
on their currents, a black-feather hovering

for months from that day forward
over the multiplying, uncountable hearts.

GOD PARTICLES

They show up after a death, arranging a face on The Shroud.
They make the waterfall fall.
They make the shine in Whitman's eye, the flies in orbit around the hungry.
Under the Alps, they lose the recent race to protons.
They make grilled peach halves over strawberry, the drizzle of honey.
They make that hand, one finger over another.
Under the Alps, they make the six-legged horse just over a rise, coming
    this way, bearing down.

THE READING LIGHT

Sometimes I remember the horse I never had,
her flanks twitching under flies in our summer barn.
I know enough about her ways to know
the long drink at the trough before we set out,
the head jerking up and down, then slipping
calmly into harness and bit. I'm riding
bareback out of the yard, past the machine shed,
past my mother's tomatoes and squash,
chickens running right and left until the dog
snarls them back. After the last corral
we're running away for good, across yellow
acres my father saves for cattle, antelope,
for walks early November under
the deepest constellation, the northern lights
surging our way just over the horizon,
coming this very night, he is sure,
if we can stay up late enough. We're running
away to the lightning-black oak
on the knuckle of a hill, stepping around
hidden bunches of cactus, the badger den,
the tipi ring from the beginning of the world,
that bedrock carved with pictures. When I lean
against the trunk, my horse pulls at wheatgrass,
and I tell her every name I know for love. One
of her eyes watches the grass. One of her brown eyes
contains me, the tree, all of the land behind.
Sometimes I remember our slow ride home
through the deep fields and dark, my ear to her mane,
my arms around her, the two of us
a black moving crescent under the moon.

Sometimes we stop at the creek for her to drink.
Sometimes we do not get home until after midnight,
the other animals barely stirring
under their roofs, each animal secret
safe for now, the reading light in the window
left on like an idea to hold in the hand
until I reach my bed, left on like every light
a man high in the sleeping plane sees, glancing
down, crossing his country in silence.

HOW TO READ A POEM

Every poem begins just before
9:00 A.M. and never ends, or the other
way around, reaching toward us
from a place we never knew, stopped
dead at our feet here and now, locked
in the day. The hardest part

is seeing where the dark began
or begins to end. All those men,
long or fetal, dropping from
the sky. All those ashen women
running in the street. Each human
vowel burned, burning, or quiet,

the sun blazing through every line
and tower. No one knows, really,
where light or evil comes from.
The moon knocks at smoke like an eye
behind the door, an eye trying
to get in. All night, tapping

grows weaker in the direction
of caesura, or the soft turn
of the sonnet's ninth line, the
poem that will make us love again.
It's a sound we might have heard once,
less than a heartbeat, a leap

as in the great haiku from hope,
or the end of hope, to knowing.

16

POSTCARD TO MYSELF FROM NEW YORK

And here I eat lamb schwarma at Mamoun's.
And here some chèvre, a baguette in the Park.
A woman sings in French, almost in tune.
A man covers his heart across the walk.

This building sprouted flowers twice a day.
That bench made a bed. These trees a forest
for good children looking to lose their way.
No one screamed. That girl found the dead boy first.

Now it's dance. Fountains turned on block-to-block
by week's end. The glide of low cloud
across the blinking roofs. We all know God
will hear the quietest prayer. A sparrow

falls. Sea wind rolls up these avenues, missing
that river of cures. Here I am, swimming.

TRACE

A last wave of him slicing
away from the pier. The last
road of him pedaling south
along the tracks.

A match of rise and fall, one
beat to the next. What makes a
good man good. The ocean and
the barren hills

survive him. What leaves no trace,
what quiet invisible flower
stitches sea and land to its
own insistence.

GUARDIAN ANGELS

After the last ones leave, Walt Whitman
still walks beside me, invisible,
blowing kisses into the ears of punks
and bankers alike, checking a lapel
for sheen and lint, tousling the hairdo
of a girl. How has it come to this,
that only one committed humanist
has not deserted? Surely I am blessed
with good air and water, and reckless trucks
do not seek me out. I was not beaten
by mother or stranger, raped by an uncle.
I was not set upon by sores. I am not
found lingering near the rails of our high bridge.

Yet I have stood at Minneopa Falls,
water falling twice, and not known how
to go on. In the deepest part of spring,
spray rose up from rocks with the roar
of falling, and I could not see beyond
my family, losing and finding their ways
over and over, losing and finding me.
Back in the city, cars go down one street
and back the next, and call it change.
Drivers look at me like ditch grass
or deer, part of the view. How has it
come to this, Americans alone
in sedans and trucks, waiting for me
to flip them off, to say something stupid
before they turn off their engines
and assault me? How has it come to this,

violence the first drug for a deadening
routine, Third Street to Broad Street to Third?

When I was eight, the first angel tapped me
on the shoulder just before sleep. Maybe
it was the way to say I didn't
need him, there in a split-level house,
Los Angeles, ocean air a balm
for anything. Even then, children stepped on
mines. I saw pictures of the swollen bellies,
flies drinking a boy's tears. We had all the right
subscriptions in those days. Maybe I didn't
need an angel to keep me lucky,
safe from TB in the dust. I had
the pink sugar cube that fought polio,
the loaves that fought hunger. I lived far away
from the reckless truck jumping sidewalks
in other parts of the world. Falling asleep,
two taps on the shoulder, maybe
it was the way to say he'd see me later.

Walt Whitman likes the bars with patios
in front, where smokers huddle since the ban,
where people drink and sometimes know a sparrow
from a finch. Even when I'm talking,
he whispers lines I won't remember. The people
roar like water. A friend wears the face
of a smoothed-down stone. Another's arm
curves into itself, a bronze leaf. Mid-summer,
we drink beer, people who know how salt
from a living ocean tastes. Walt Whitman
puts his hand over my wife's breast. He tells me

her heart speaks my name to his fingers.
I am telling her about my day. His other hand
waves at me from behind her head.

What would it take to ask the angels back,
to interrogate their motive, to double-check
those days I knew them near—a back alley
off Western in Seattle, that tumble under
a storm-driven wave? Maybe I had
left them. Were they the home ground
I could stray from? Would it take real
desperation to get them to return?
Would that seem contrived? Whitman takes no stand
on this score, tugging at strands of his beard.
He has had all he will take of me
this afternoon, even as he mimics
the posture of another self: Walt Whitman
the mortal, days after his final stroke.
He tries to lift an arm, settling instead
on what he can see. The stitching
of his quilt. The coat on a chair-back. Sunlight
waking up the airborne dust of his room.

RECOVERY

God works in material ways.

—overheard at a café

Even as ocean water boils
to nothing, as granite stumbles
to grit. Even as the oak
give up their roiling orange to duff,
and salmon, silver, turn from foil
to red, to creek-bottom black.

Even now the sutured heartbeat
louder than rooms, a kind of green
beyond the glass, out the door.
So many ways to live again,
taking in breath, feeling this stone
through a shoe. So many dear

departed ones who might have stayed
but loved mystery more. The day
is for repair, the sutured
heart will say. Tear and tear again.
The angel does not hide from you.
Her sharp blade waits for the hour.

GOING-TO-THE-SUN HIGHWAY

Without fear we parked the car on the thin
bulge beside the cliff and crossed to where
the glacier filled our Mickey Mouse or Elbow Taproom

pints, whatever we had brought to taste
what came out of the sky ten, a hundred
years before. If it was Sunday, we'd gone

to Mass in Kalispell, then brunched
at the Jordan Café, where a waiter,
regardless of group or size, memorized

the order. We'd driven north through narrowing
gorges to the Park, then up the U-shaped
valley on Going-to-the-Sun, the long

slow string peppered with rockfall, slicked
with melt, toward Logan Pass. Fifty years now,
and the family can't remember grizzly prints

or eagles plucking char from Lake MacDonald,
only the forgiven carload, dozy
from the road, renewed by the Body and Blood

of Christ, restored by breakfast, slaking
its thirst in a field of scree, the water
cold as we'd ever known, a taste simple

as granite, the sun beating on us
at 6000 feet, and a waterfall
being born under our shoes, crossing its first

of four borders before it died, a thousand
miles from there, in the sea.

2. *Moving the Dead River West*

THE MARTIAN POET

The Martian poet of his generation
does not promote himself as such. He does
not pout when the host does not present his
check by noon on the day of their meeting.
He is a grateful guest, far from the desert
that is both home and sorrow, modest in
his needs without fawning. He does not wear
his anger like the veteran his medals.
He is not proud of being bruised by his
birth, as a rich man is made smug by his
father's money. He does not wear Eguzh,
the Neruda of Mars, in his poems
like the lawyer dressing in denim. He
does not carry his frown like the man who
carries false teeth in his pocket only
to smile in darkness. He does not promote
himself as such.

The Martian poet of his generation
is more like Q, who doesn't need me to
mention his name. He has come 141
million miles to read you his poem about
the sad, drunken brother in the middle
of the night. He will scramble eggs for you
if you stop by his rust-colored house. He
will help you wash dishes if he visits
yours. He wears his Martian body like a

manta ray wavering over coral, like
a bear hovering over his bones. If he
growls at you, it will be because he is
proud of his teeth and the bad breath of bears
and the stink of brine—all emblems of the
higher qualities of Martians. It will be
compliment beyond measure
that he thinks enough of you to show real feeling
rather than to wear a mood like the fraying
sweater he put on one afternoon
below zero reading Zerx, the Vallejo
of Mars, and forgot ever to take off.

The Martian poet of his generation
does not make everything of what he had
nothing to do with—although he could, with
the ease of angels, match another's horror
with his own, even as he erased it
in the dark of your four hands.

MOUTHS

He hung over the house like a cloud,
watching each of them walk in and out,
the ice dams huge, then melting to nothing,
the chimney puffing its little mouth.

In summer he could nearly see through
tangled beams into the upstairs rooms
where his children filled journals or hummed songs
while he and his wife, moving below,

made bread or cooked a meal. He could see
life going on like this, pinned to sky
like a butterfly to cork. Storms passed through
with places to be, didn't ask why

there's more going away than coming home
down below, why the cellar brimming
with radon turns up sharp and clear at this
altitude, even as a voice dims

at those eaves, and last light flares orange
at roofline, every wish in its bed.

"NORTHUMBRIAN MINER AT HIS EVENING MEAL"

—a photograph by Bill Brandt, 1937

He eases small tendons from the bone
quick as she foresees the coffee gone
from white cup, dark bread and chop from their white
plate, the butter, sugar, milk withdrawn

to a counter, the table clear now
for the black body to be laid down,
Belgian lace under, around it, his last
socks drying in front of, years ago,

a holiday they took once to the sea.

THE END OF A LONG WINTER NORTH
IN THE NORTHERN HEMISPHERE

Out my window, thin as an incision,
trucks have left tidal waves of sand. Pablo,
they're preparing the square for the games,
for volleyball and sumo wrestling in suits
full of air. Already I hear a goose-stepping
army in bikinis swarming up the long hill
to mix virgin daiquiris by the rusty
fountain. I can barely see the long string
of balloons held aloft like helium cysts.
I can barely hear myself in the animal
grunt a student makes when he spikes the ball
south.

Pablo, find the green in this dark,
the jungle heat to close over so many
happy Swedes. I know, I am the beetle
stuck by the jaw to leaf-bottom, I am
the worm that will destroy the canopy.
Still, I need you to explain the bagpipes
coming this way through the woods, and the kilts
flying up regularly, and the perfume
of sex now steadily on the wind,
and birds singing as from the inside
of coffeepots. They're throwing javelins
and shovels and bookcases and the passports
of missing diplomats. They're lighting charcoal.
Very soon there will be meat on the fire
and the spray of cola.

"FLOYD AND LUCILLE BURROUGHS, HALE COUNTY, ALABAMA"

—a photograph by Walker Evans, 1936

Where the floor planks go, he goes.
Where the wall planks go, she goes.
Where the bare feet begin, both

through this door frame to supper,
out to old fields of the earth.
Where his wrist holds together,

where her fingers meet their next
hinge, a place where each second
side of them loves to meet itself.

THE HOUSE

Nudged into an inner wall, witness
to every squabble, there was a nest
where grief lay its eggs. Their footsteps led there,
even walking away. Sorry joists

bulged like ribs. Across humming, ancient
wires, their house talked and talked, the present
they gave themselves for a miracle birth
of something flying, tired, out their chests.

NEAR ROSLIN INSTITUTE, MIDLOTHIAN, SCOTLAND

—birthplace of the cloned sheep Dolly

Under the groined roofs of Rosslyn Chapel,
a man plays bagpipes in stone while Abraham
sharpens his knife. Across the lintel falls
King Darius, asleep, dragon attacks
imminent at every pillar despite
the best wishes of carved cleric or king,
despite corporal works of mercy, prayers
the ploughman might send up, or husband, wife,
carpenter, gardener, sportsman, child on knees
next to its own skeleton, the farmer—

each too wrapped by Vice or The Dance of Death
to be saved. Blessed are they, then, for stories
telling themselves upward from stone. Past the mouths
of snakes, a dog leads the blind man to glory.
Doves with olive leaves sweep over his head.
A seated lady prays for him. A warrior
battles, a monk drinks for the coming crown.
Christ is dying everywhere for the dead.
And near each stained glass an angel hovers
in its light with scroll, cross, or book—open

at one niche, closed at the next—the story
turning inward, outward, all in color
blazing through saints. No wonder, too, history
must reject this place. Its business to suffer
more than believe, to act larger than hope,
and smaller, it makes the counter-legends

to the Grail locked in these foundations. It
needs to repeat itself, first to last cup
and back, while two fields away, quite decent
men walk a lamb into light without origin.

KITCHEN

How is it, cutting
pink grapefruit, the bloody halves
rock a moment on

the board, shining up all
the way to the table, all

the little rooms scooped
out, moving your direction
on the spoon, and you

hardly notice what's going
inside, those hundreds of tears,

hundreds of dams near
breaking, newspaper glaring
back in its dumb way,

your mouth open, the city
moving the dead river west.

THE WOMEN OF LOCKERBIE

After the explosion and the hail
of fire and linen, after hot steel
cooled on the ground, they buried each neighbor
or son, undertook the terrible

reunion that began with quiet heaps
of travelers' clothing left on each stoop
by the coroner. In their own kitchens
they picked bits of hair, bone from the slope

of a shoulder yoke, they bleached out soot,
perfume of fear, their tired Scottish dirt
before they washed the clothes for a last time,
dried them on a line in west wind, brought

each thing back inside for the pressing,
the folding, the packing in tissue
before all was sent back in parcels
marked for shipping to the grieved ends of earth.

3. *Body Turn to Rain*

VIOLENCE
_____

When she said time, she meant her grandmother's mink coat, still torn
    from the formal-dinner wars, holding its breath under the clear
    laundry bag in a dark closet.

When she said earth, she meant the moon under each fingernail, the
    different stories they could tell about the body.

When she said sky, she meant everything changeable and above her.

When she said soul, she meant everything beyond sky or closer, here
    inside the first world.

When she said evil, she meant the foot rolling the girl into the ditch, the
    two-beat pause before the lie, the hand writing the executive order,
    the easy stale air she breathes before turning away.

When she said love, she meant the reservoir emptying, the rush of water
    down the canyon, the eucalypti, cars, and broken households of the
    rich jostling toward the basin. In the one-story homes lower down,
    human beings could only dream of the love coming their way,
    driving them and animals to rooftops where in a rush of air the
    yellow sling would come to find them, to lift them into the dim room
    held aloft by each slicing blade.

The story of you came out of the lake to find the tree covered with
    initials.

What does the spirit know, really, following its little song westward to
    the receding edge of glacier.

What could the eye follow into the folding stone, the thread of light
    lingering in mica, fire at the cool center of basalt.

The woman became water again when the car and the house and
    the dog roaming in the yard all turned to her at the same time in
    order to grow larger than themselves.

We wanted this all along. We wanted the phone ringing outside of
    history. The wind of our dance along the cliff edge where the
    old prophet stopped his singing.

Say something, we said. Tell us the country your tongue came from,
    and its manner of forests. Tell us the name of wind behind your
    eyes. Tell us what new star has named your fingertips already,
    what river they follow back to the billion-year-old heart.

IMPOSSIBLE DREAM

Wherein he moves to the city,
capital of nightmare, crouching

on the stained pavement without bread
or weapon, even as the thug

begins his circle, and taxis
blur to yellow, voice and body

rising, saying, *Kill me. Feed this.*

APHASIAC

Welcome for coming.
Please be advised along the rails of the guided ship.
The first of every month and you were the smartest one.
Out of the heavens spun above us just like that.
The liver throbbed a basket of lilies a garbage-filled cathedral.
Please sit yourself home.
We have only begun the cave wall blooming finally with animals.

HISTORY

If only the chair could talk, overstuffed with our pauses, or the window
  that let us breathe that afternoon the car ran off the road.
If only the Japanese beetle meandering in the overhead fixture, if only
  the world-traveling orange. Or the song on the radio, if only it could
  talk about the equatorial village where the songwriter was born, if
  only it could remake the heat at noon, the fish coming in in the bellies
  of small boats, the arm muscles of the one fisherman unloading—
  how, the first time, the woman looked at them.
If only the shirt button. If only the eye and hook. If only wind blowing
  inland, through every kind of door. If only the opening and closing eyes
  of sickness. If only lily blossoms by day, by night. If only the painted
  center line in the desert suddenly jittering, swaying like a snake.
The wave says its name on the shore, always one language to the next,
  one ocean edge to the other, under heaving bows, through drifting
  counties of salt, garbage, and kelp, over the unrecorded earthquakes
  far below.
And now the tallest building climbs into the mouth of sky.
And now the three bones of the ear pass their news to the body.
Still, the letter blows unopened off the bench. Huge stones run their
  faltering line across the field. Men and women in a factory are
  listening to machines, assembling cigars, plastic toys, pickup trucks.
  What they make makes a word, that and the hand reaching at night
  for another. The phone will not ring. The house will write their
  history as they sleep.

My life isn't that important, but I remember that afternoon seeing you run away and only get so far. You cried on the lawn next to your lawn. The high hedge grew mountainous between them.

You'd wrapped your things in a bandanna and tied them to the end of a stick. Behind you, the shrub bent with its load of pomegranates. On the ground, one of the globes had torn open, spilling its red tears.

I left my Chinese elm and crossed the street to sit down with you. The man who owned that lawn, the man we hardly ever saw, flew a biplane along the coast of North Africa. He smuggled guns for Tunisian rebels. He had ripped off the ears of temporary captors. He had left scorpions in the limp gloves of spies. We wondered if his curtains would suddenly open and we'd see him again at his picture window, like that time he sat there all month, his arm in plaster, his forehead stitched, smoking cigarette after cigarette and grinning as he exhaled, grinning as the smoke snaked back into his nose.

We lay on our backs, the grass itching our necks. Now there was the sky deep blue with autumn, and now there was the problem of how to go back home.

In your bandanna was a pair of socks, a change of underwear, the missal you received for your First Communion, a Werewolf comic book, a Mars bar, a pencil with a broken tip, a travel comb, a Stardust Hotel ash tray you used to keep coins in before you ran away, one three-cent postcard stamp, a piece of chalk taken from Mrs. McGovern's classroom, a Charles Atlas ad snipped from the back of another comic book, a length of yarn, a skate key.

Now there was the problem of how to go back home. All your things spread out like items at a sad picnic. Under them, a paisley pattern rippled across the uneven altitudes of grass.

You broke the Mars bar in half and shared it. There were lines on your cheeks where tears had cut trails through the dust. You gathered your bundle together. You broke the stick in half and threw it under the hedge. You made me swear I never saw you cry. We crossed our hearts. The green of that street scratched us. The blue of that street made us shiver. A stranger might have watched through the drapes. I crossed my heart. My life doesn't add up to much, but that was the moment I betrayed you, even though it took all these years until now to see it through.

All those angry months leaving the self until the jungle cover opened onto a path winding, like a narrow Incan trail, into the hills.

All those years of forgiveness, mustard blossoms in the field behind his first home. All the fields. The homes.

Every knuckle broken, every eye bruised, every rasping breath queuing to make the rosary that would circle back to him.

North to south to north, all the swallows traveling one continent to the next, slaves of spring, waving their S-patterns in the air at each return.

Every horse in a yellow field. Every first home.

All those years like an ancient craftsman pounding the things around him into the shape of beads. All this before he came to resemble a station of the cross. The scene of an accident. The emptiness where someone had just stood or something had just happened before it moved on. Every bead an artery.

Every bead an artery. Every artery a star. Every star climbing behind the rock face just beyond the mountain ruin. Every star leaving the line of its passing behind, thread of a veil, lit strand of a rope, the sky road that would lead him to the edge, but no further, of dark space without him.

IMPOSSIBLE MODESTY

Wherein the man removes his shoes,
his clothes, lifetimes of desire

hung now on the chair back, bodiless,
the door to the next world opening

as if to dark space without pole
or gravity, as if to dark

inside a mouth that will not speak.

He made a wish, finally, the veins of his hand run to the sea.

He made a wish the red moon cruel.

He talked to the home on the short street ending at a circle. He smelled oleander leaves, the dust falling there from sky. He talked to the Chinese elm, to the ghost of a white dog, the outlawed incinerator, to the versions of boy walking in and out the door.

He walked into an empty church next to the ocean. Each candle flickered in wet air, a kind of speech. A kind of speech, he prayed to no one at the altar. He bowed to the polished stone.

He walked, finally, across sand, past living and dying gulls, past flea, past marbles of tar, to the thumbnail moons of foam.

He tasted their salt. Not iron, not evil, not a long disappointed message from lunar dark. Just a mineral he could bathe in, those two vowels only an angel—rubbing two halves of a man together—knows how to say.

The shallow bay, rippling earlobe of the 1000-foot-deep lake, pulled on itself like a clue in charades, tugged like boats in their slips. It scooped the quietest decibel out of midnight sky and eased it toward another darkness, where the brain waited to translate. At the bottom of the lake lived 100-year-old sturgeon hovering over broken tackle and aluminum cans, two dozen pairs of lovers, a lost F-9 jet. At the bottom of the brain, all these things listened to radio music streaming from the next galaxy.

The trees never spoke, actually. The car drove straight through their lives, what might have been the richest of conversations, but wind did all the talking around their surfaces, and over the curve of hood, and along the knife edge of window the man had rolled down just enough to hear the world's velocity in its own language.

Whatever repose existed, falling rock always sought another, down the cliffside, in and out of the grassy borrow pit, across the shoulder, into the lane of traffic. All of this when no one was looking.

Just outside the city, night turned orange, orange as the light behind his eyelids on the brightest day at the beach.

In the town square, the man turned a slow circle until he came back finally to where he began. In the movie inside his head at that exact moment, one of two women came into view as he finished. If he made another circle, the other waited at the end. He loved these two equally once, on water, in woods, over the long highway that took him anywhere, dodging the fallen rock. Now they live as compass points, single degrees of imagined reunion, points on a circle inside a square, breathing the orange air.

The morning he died throbbed in his ears until suddenly it was noon. Inside his chest, desert animals came out of hiding to drink. His eye, to the loved one, looked like a blue ring laid over an immaculate beach where, just last night, it had rained.

Along the banks of the estuary at that same moment, a plover turned its
ear to the sand, listening for tiny crabs. The trickle of water, what
was left of the rush down the mountains, walked quietly toward the
crash of wave. A human being tried to listen to this. Not even the
bird heard the whisk of thread as it was pulled from whatever had
stitched the man to earth.

IMPOSSIBLE TRANSCENDENCE

Wherein, like the Buddha, he lets
go into the river of non-

attachment, her gone, them gone, all
the gravity of suffering re-

calculated for age, baggage,
the wild crush of epiphanies

roasting the unfolding flower.

He kept driving, each storefront a shoulder-to-shoulder forest he couldn't
see around.

All those miles down the boulevard, numbers counting down by twos.

And the field opening where the buildings end, and light settling over
the lengthening eye.

And wind across the tops of bluestem and the lives of insects.

And all animals in the grass, even birds, moving in their own ways under
the sun.

And on the horizon, something like his shadow walking, something small
as a daytime star against the blue moving up and down over the far
line of earth.

IN MILOSZ'S ROOM

What can one man pass on to the other beyond the afterimage of his
   disappearance.
As in this room, where years ago the one man lay, never far from his loss,
   the skeleton of a bird marauding the night sky outside the glass.
As in this room, now, the other man dressing the heron against cedar
   bough in daylight, constructing the narrative of its solitude, counting
   the beats of the heart.
Somewhere on a road they might have met, walking in different directions
   from similarly ruined towns. Both men escaped with their lives. Both
   shouldered emptiness and blessing.
In the museum of this room, both slept troubled.
Looking up from the pillow, they spent nights drawing whole cities on
   a ceiling canvas dedicated to blankness.
They made separate pacts, finally, with silence. As terms of the agreement,
   one is allowed only a handful of phrases for the remainder of his life,
   a company of ghosts pointing to bare kingdoms inside him. For the
   other, the wind of the other man's leaving, the smell of that room,
   as after candles have been blown out, and the radiator still ticks with
   heat, the room filling with familiar darkness, poised, a possible lung.

He can't help but notice the thick outer wall humming like a tuning fork,
   the radiator ticking its final heat.

All the castles ruined but this one, in the kingdom of evening, no hope
   again of sleep when the ghosts rehearse their lines in either ear.

Once there was an orchard in the old empire, the sun just coming up,
   dew shining on the apple boughs. A creek lit the first fire as a boy
   walked beside it to the chattering school.

Outside, nighthawks slice the dark above the gorge. Beyond these drawn
   curtains, windows rattle in the weather. Below the wind, the river
   untangling its dead, even as the surface freezes.

What of that table in this dark where he will work the next morning.

There's blood on the nib of his pen, and empty train cars returning to a
   small village. Bread and fish have been left at the door, enough to get
   by on, and memory offers up its own wine, or antidote to wine, along
   those long corridors of want.

He turns from side to side. Two angels, one of them fallen, whisper in
   his ears.

He turns from side to side, listening to their confessions. Heaven exists,
   they both say, though one of them is lying. Heaven exists, they both
   say, and the boy still walks there, the school already in flames, the
   smoke just coming up over the line of sycamores, a curiosity that will
   burn in him all the poisoned, blèssed days ahead.

IMPOSSIBLE WILDERNESS

Wherein the hand persuades the key
and pomegranate at once, fire

jumps upward from heartwood, deadfall,
the stone hearth floor, her voice every

good night gone sounding a thousand
miles from any mouth, any mouth,

the red rind tearing them open.

Maybe we have come finally that far where the afternoon of lazy reading
in the heat no longer matters, only planting perennials near the
billion-year-old gneiss, only buying grain without stone, grain
without its hound's tooth of blood.

We could try to move back to the last city. From the bridge, we could see
the backs of trout then, rippling green as green water, nosing toward
the sea. The horse met us at the back fence, taking off the tops of
our roses. We fed it apples anyway. Our child lay new to us on new grass.

Maybe this street has already tricked its neighbors, routed them elsewhere
toward oblivion of pine or static. Somehow we have come finally
far enough to know we're hearing this intersection for the first time,
without echo. The car driving by carries teenagers talking, talking,
each on the way to some ultimate damage. Chickadees tick in the elm.

Or maybe the map, the first dreamscape, made a place for us here. After
the woman had the house built, after homes surrounded the
farmstead, after covenants against Jews and Indians, after oak,
maple, and plum set their roots, after the next woman died ironing
in the basement, after one across the street lost her daughter, after
the man down the block his arm, after the trolley disappeared right
in front of them, after a tornado three streets away, after the rage
one summer burning the near part of town, after flooding creek bed
and river, after music came down from the sky one warm, humid
night, the insects humming.

After a long winter, neighbors sit on their front steps. Others are doing
the same thing on the other side of the world.

The world gave us wind, the breath between human beings. It gave us
the road shoulder anywhere on earth, a place between the blue lines
of a map.

What do we say to the others when their rice reaches our plate. What do
they say to us, wearing shorts and shirts we recognize. What do they
say to us, waving their greeting, the day we march, a slow green wall,
into their veins.

THE INVISIBLE WEDDING «««« 1984

WHALESHIPS IN WINTER QUARTERS
AT HERSCHEL ISLAND

—a painting by John Bertoncini

If I skate out of white, even my voice
fades. I can't remember the cave
where the sound of me tripled into bats
hanging in dark upper cracks, hanging
onto phrases each would repeat to me
forever. I come home out of range of myself.
Across a frozen body, blue and blue
valleys wind into blue and give up their blue
to sky. Here is the unforgivable
deceit: the lie of charcoal roofs, that lives
go on beneath the smoke and recreation.
I have skated away and am missing.

Northwest of light, perfect color of discovered
stone. Beyond being empty, the hand.
I could die now, easily enough. Away
from the actual, the mad dog, shipboard
crucifixions, away from innings of misery
on ice, cold star even years ago
just a hand's length too far away to reach.
The day lights its blurred candle in the south.
I am missing and am missing the chimes
morning and recollection become. Time
after time, the smokehouse gives way to receding
land. A dark chapel opens, the hidden
heartlocked music waiting to begin.

AT HOOVER DAM

A boy is as young as ten feathers
that wouldn't burn,
as the chopping of wood
spring mornings, the gaze five miles
out of Boulder City falling
long and down. Over drowned sage,
over hill cuts tracking
the dream of hands—the secret den
already filled—water there
backed up far to the north,
and in the scream of gorge, in desert blue
lifting, a river went on
changed though still the motion
of a century's snow,
what the mountain chose to lay down.

Though he died there, though that storm
on another lake turned owls
loose at noon, the heart draws in
its flurry of doves, its black fire.
Draws, though a hill sags
at the marriage of waters in all places
raining, though a woman closes
on her garden of flint,
though earth, fern, the split rock
of green lines, though the boy
saw stars with his name,
wakes to find the city gone.

You do not dream the passion of trout,
short breaths of cedar.
The woman who loves counts lines in the eyes
of another, and you are
the one familiar to a sunken road,
to bad light honest for its fault. If trees blow away,
folded ground. If elk vanish, whistles
gone the way of song
and those who brought you here. Nothing
matters like a road. No one cares
the sky died overnight
responsible for sin. Here,
a blast of magpies. Grin of concrete
four wars out of tune. Out that spillway
the tumble rush a boy
heard faintly, the wailing now, a praise
of things about to disappear.

CLIMBING THE NINE HILLS

A hundred thousand times
the treasure loses
meaning, you move out
on the great road: guarding
your loss, choosing not to pursue.

In a high meadow
poverty and wrens, a horse
and its natural pact with fields.
The way a new shoot
spreads, a way of watching
the field fill out.

Seven days again, return.
Riches of the old life
down below,
before a highway moved you.
These hills bear the memory
of thunder
if you listen. Over stumps
and deadfall, into the perfect
pitch of chert, the same
thoughts travel:
I carry the best of you away,
you carry the heart of me through stone.

SATURDAY IN MIDWINTER

The house still too cold, on and off. Lifetimes
from now I might wonder for the second
time why, for instance, the overhead lights
always dim, or seem to dim, after illness.
Or why it's the gentle knees that give out,
are the last to recover. Six hundred
miles from here, on the Washington coast,
a wave from ten times that distance away
spends its message on the beach. Boulders,
in their fashion, say nothing. Hemlocks
rising up a creek bed make no special
move in return. Nothing is out of order.
On the Washington coast, as here, the stories
are telling themselves. The sick man's
sky moves slowly over us. Rain falls
for the first time in a month. When I walk
from one window to the next, I watch
not only the second lawn without snow,
not only the lilac half-heartedly dormant,
but a second sky: a walking man's gray
barely more than two arms' lengths above me.
It might serve the view to have a healthy
fern near the window, to take note
in seeing it of my chest clearing or eyes
obeying their focus. But I won't lie.
Here, as at the other pane of glass,
I have to lean sometimes, the house
propping me up as the rain falls, necessary,
and the west grows whiter with latecoming
clouds of snow.

SWAINSON'S HAWK

On a Sunday like this, a front moving in,
prairie grass bent to its toes
in the velocity of air, some fields being tilled,
some snow melting fast on the north-facing coulee-sides,
the wind does the hawk's flying for it.

Gophers are out. The prairie dogs are out.
I fly north in my steel
to the Fort Peck where feathers burn in drought.
Prairie dogs pop up from rye grass
on the shoulder of the road,

and the Swainson's hawk is hovering.
A tall shadow closes over another.
I fly north in my steel toward burning color,
dust storm, alkali. The space between us is more
than wheat turned to wheat grass turned to ruin.

The wind does the hawk's flying for it.

CHRISTMAS EVE

Began blue over the near hill, cold
from the clear night storms had left them.
They brought mums to Holy Cross, and in their own steam
knelt at the Mulica graves, last
leaves of poplar rusted beside them.
It was clouding. Began to snow on the way
back to fasting and the midnight Mass.
My grandmother rubbed and rubbed her bad hands.

South always came blue, even in rain.
Even if the ocean turned winter
for a morning, south came always blue, better
late than never. We were a family
by then. Los Angeles our dead uncles, a green home
left behind. The new house on the hill
kept quiet about the history of grass—
the field we filled—but some of us

could hear it, rolled on without knowing
toward the wave-sliced cliff where the story
told itself. Christmas Eve we spent alone
without cousins. It darkened early.
When I was young I looked for the comet,
but I saw only stars, and each one
was brighter, each one red and blue
if you stared. I never knew to ask

about Pocatello. They might not have talked.
After all, it was the future coming: my loud
cousins, the immortal ham,
what was left of us for beginning again.

TOWARD NEW WEATHER

Bad times: drought, Egil's dog had mange, the white
lilies fell like hair around our house. Crows
gave us up, let the corn dwarfs holler
on their own for hail, dull wind. It's the kitchen,
midnight, Father says *Leave it all* and feels
the last scotch burn. Lost calves low far away.
The mountain cries for snow, drawing sheets

of lightning to its back. Father dreams the green
of moss on northern shingles, coiling dust
between his fingers. The rest of us
wonder from our corners of the evening, this
table. The next thing he says will be *Move*,
and it will be Pocatello then, bench land
and always rain, alfalfa that swallows the cows.

This is our second pestilence.
When Mother died the dying lilac bloomed
for days before a hot wind browned
the flowers, spread them over the field.
Everything goes wrong then. For some reason
Kansas burns, a well bottoms out. Father
laughs, leaves the sky to itself. We drive west,

and now he is singing. Now he is singing
If a person don't have but two teeth
they look better if they're close together.

A GLIDER TAKES OFF FROM THE CLIFF

Wind blew away before you knew the space
behind it. A far hill crowded sky
that night, and stars, stars named only by
the foolish, whined in their narrow routes.
Mother didn't hate you, nor the cauldron
of ash turned over at your birth. Low light
meant the first fire loosed upon the mountain,
and when she looked she saw her own smoke,
gone before she ever knew your name.

Head-stained or dead, you lost all companions.
Gulls flew away because they knew the walk
of dying, because ghosts meant a thing
unfinished, haze in the air means lame.
The cat you found wasn't born then. The elm
you pruned turned its best thoughts down. Somewhere
grew a heart you could live with, but for now
you heard none, walked dizzy in the leaves:
afraid to pray, afraid of remaining the same.

Give yourself time and a day unwinds,
the line of snow peas burning past a lawn.
Your walk brought the stone to life. The palm took
dove after dove for keeps, while children—
too late to go home—lay down in their shadow
and slept. Give yourself days and the gulls die
young. A glider takes off from the cliff
and skies rush forward to meet him, a wave
forms his deepest dream. Stars too foolish to name
resemble beach at night, and red tide, deeper

than wings, looks forward to the glider's
drop, fall toward a wave of the moon.

You thought yourself well then. Sunflowers
threw the first light of morning. Corn turned in on
their eternities of silk. If the hill sank
you wouldn't have noticed, nor the ridge
turned suddenly to fire. Out of ash
it wasn't prayer that saved you. Not midnight
thrush, not tar or music, not the river
full of voices three months past the freeze.
You were not you. You were all
you ever remembered. At the same cliff, bunch grass
rallied in a wind. Grass was different before.
Now it holds. Gulls tilt out, and the ocean holds.

MARCH

Sculling a thin lake
Cold with trout, last month I walked
Here: a narrow sky.

Snow fell bending north and once,
For an hour, vertically,

Soft without its crutch.
I swept an icy path clean,
Boots scuffing the lake—

Watched that dying world change once
Into the living middle

I walked then, row now,
Atmospheres above, below,
Breathed on and breathing.

Gulls veer away from rising
Fish yet meet at the first kiss

Of air. Each bank takes
Or sends its small tide and wind.
North to south, driftwood

Accomplishes a new life
Between the others: oars pulled

To lead me backward
Past the regret of muscle,
Heart, impulse, mind. Here

Water makes way for me. Air
Makes way. My wet hand. This boat.

Remove not the old landmark; and enter not into the field of the fatherless.

—*Proverbs 23:10*

The scarecrow never knew clouds
from the next criminal bird. We forgave it.
The sun that time of year sprawled out
below a thunderhead, turned its thoughts
beyond Japan. One day I wanted a heron
for a pet, but there were bass to fake
with rubber worms. There were cows
long gone in alfalfa, and Ninepipe fat
with weed, with coots I was afraid I'd look like.

Jackie was some bird, you'd say. *All bones,*
you said, *so thin he blew away.* He did not.
I knew they found him in Post Creek, just below
the dam. Belly-up and shining
like some perch we'd filled with air. The scarecrow
couldn't help being dumb: I tore its legs off
and plowed the spinach under.
I got whipped. I tracked deer that morning
as Ninepipe, and the shore was like a boy.
It held and let go, held and blew away.

July dried up our ponds. A marsh hawk died
in midair, and for weeks its ghosts drew circles
on our field. I didn't care. Mother
knew songs to bring rain, and she sang them,
though the tree line stayed scorched as before.
I fished above the dam, where bass had run to—

saw a bear rip a root from stone, chasing
down a scent. I had to grow up
somehow. A tree was ageless. Rocks can never live
until you skip them. I forgive you, Father.

After jade the color of my eyes, stone
elephants and medieval prayer
in wood and oil, we step outside,
hunch our backs through the Japanese garden
blooming something all the time, rest
on an arched bridge above
lily and carp, the faces we own today
giving themselves back to water.
On the way to Natural History
you stop. Down a lane the chalk
body of a man on pavement, the crime
we don't reconstruct. We walk on instead.
The ocean's not far, and its wind
comes with us, through eucalyptus, over lawn
the color of someone else's
envy. Everyone's guilty but the orchestra.
They haven't played since June.

It's a scene from our past: the wattled
hut and clay jug, fire handed down
since you or I was born. In the tanks
our same dream under glass. The lantern fish,
blinded by its own light,
moves green, dark, moves green and away.
Five miles down, we'd leave too,
swim to be always leaving, pass what we found
out our gills.
It's dark after the blue whale.
We drive south toward where those lights
thin. Down the coast without

moon or star, down a line
of breath between what rises,
what falls down into sea. Sculpture
hasn't failed us. This night,
endlessly autumn, opens up.
That voice we hear is water. Your heart
is what came this far.

MARRIAGE IN WINTER

This is not sadness, it is a lake.
Holes in the sky are not ice
crying but the fish's eye on weather, an early
death. Sparrows love you
when you dump your trash. A cougar
seen three years before returns:
it doesn't love you, but loud summer's
gone and you're the only one
who draws the animals out. This is not friendship,
it is blood. Murder won't belong
while the tenth-year freeze
goes on and no one can drown until April.

Set-lines hedge against not sleeping. Snow blind
at a Z of shuffled boots, a path
leading north beyond the islands, you Our Father
the cutthroat, pray the whitefish smoked
before the animals know. Later,
come to table, this evening lifts from the same range
where winter rose, sent out
talk and breeze over the waves. You'll auger
new holes soon. You'll sadden other lives
for hunger and still remain
blameless as weed, a blameless fox,
crosser of the ice.

You will not be less alone. You won't be
lonely, because sadness
is not this lake, even if you are widowed,
even if you are matched. When your wife arrives

she finds you groom to more
than your simple wedding. You point out to her
the tracks of morning drinkers at the holes,
low-slung clouds on that irrelevant
peninsula. You tell her you could love each other.
By dinner, she believes. Both of you believe in
snapped air, the largest raven
of the season. Winter does not part,

it is a marriage.
This lake is not land, it is a going on and on.

ASSURANCES

The bad ground flowers once the house turns home.
Twice a day, it's lovely when the finches
bare their heads. Winter gave our skin back,
winter raised these rocks to light. Our yard

has memory. Yards resemble lakes at high water,
and they recall the gestures
of weather, the home like an island at their shore.

We shouldn't forget ourselves. A crow
won't pretend to have a name, and elm more dignity
than shape. We till sorrow into earth
but bad ground's home for only wind to move on.

We shouldn't hope for home. You died once.
I carried your ashes past the farthest
of your journeys, sent you on your way.
When I died, someone said my name and not a breath

faltered. Not breath of wind, which
changed my shape. Not trees, which turn ash
to their color. I was a day's hurricane
away from you. You were the expanse I flew through.

We never met. We meet now only where
our deaths cross, and that is good:
never did our names burn lovelier than eyes.

RETURNING TO THE MIDDLE

It was long after you died.

I brought you back here, stooped down
and left your ashes in the lake.
They spread out like a cloud
the day after rain, wading out toward the middle

with each new boat wake
or whisper of storm crashing on the shore.
You would have loved that March,
that one bright afternoon. We were alone,

there were cutthroat snatching flies,
and all I could think of
turned blue in my memory, even the voice
you saved to break the most fragile

of silences. Blue lake, blue sky—
fish blurring blue and you talking
one day trolling for salmon,
talking as our boat

strayed toward the middle
about leaving each other by illness
or circumstance: being sad about that,
not wanting to be wrongly sad.

We never came near catching our limit.
If it was a day like many others,
we passed the cliff paintings
on the way back to camp. Easing the boat

close to the granite wall,
we counted ocher bison for the hundredth time,
the thirty or so red strokes
without clear reference. The one eye this painted man

faces east forever
is returning forever to the lake.
His gaze left what you left, turns out
toward a small branch and drift of weed:

the feeding and draining river made visible.

SAMARAS

A month-long snow under grosbeaks feasting
in our elm. What they don't get hangs on
or falls, June wings, to our yard. What falls
fills the cup of tulip, cave of iris,
nooks among the marigold leaves, any
daylight broken through our elm and falling
to grass. In the wine glass left out in rain,
a paper-covered seed bulges and sprouts.
And the huge-billed birds—they gorge themselves
profanely on these wafers that will save
no one, but could, that do answer hunger,
then greed, and keep on falling from the tree.
In the wine glass, rain disappears, a root
fails its ground. When seeds fly, we can see wind.

THE INVISIBLE WEDDING

After the lake dropped, well past the songs
rain whispered on a last day of grief,
we went down, down to the creek bed, where clouds
retire. What did we care for stiff wings
dragonflies had left, or for stone
washed over, the memory of sumac. Our sky
was narrower then. Your hand swept the gorge
and its roiling poplars. I fished
until I forgot beginning, and we slept there
on a dry bank that wouldn't stop its talk:
the creek full of names, that bank
which in our dream we took the shape of.

Dreams don't retire from the light we see,
from the shuffling of rock-flakes loosened
as we sashay down a grade. We owned
a farm here before any other white.
We grew anything edible, and this gorge
spread flat toward the south, giving space
for the vines, shade for the cluster
of peas. In our dream, we lose it all.
Green rises up, and keys fly away
with the candles. The sod house flowers:
thistles and chamomile. There are no clouds
to speak of. We are not supposed to regret.

What did we care for animals passing through
that night. The hare fed, drinking near
our sleep. Flies hatched over and over again
from sand, and the owl cooled down by gliding

through the tunnel over creek. We were
not there. On the last day of grief, we turned
invisible to all but those like us.
We were histories, re-arrived too late.
It was all we could do to sweep our hands
forever. To fish, to always forget
the beginning. We didn't care to regret. We were
here. Something was going on. We didn't know.

CROSSOVER

In the year of the comet, light
fell through our windows blue
as the palest sky, shafts of light
all our wondering had
turned toward: those disappearances
of dust and smoke
finally made clear, columns of white
two flies would angle through, the grace
light brought in which invisible
wishes, lost objects found themselves,
were seen for the first time
as real, able to
reflect, breathable as air.

All those years we slept
with curtains open to a sky
revolving in our dream.
In the midst of downed stars, a crowd
scene unlike anything
we would have ever imagined,
the comet—the idea
of it fixed as perennial
blooming—slept with us too,
and we were alone with ourselves
and with what comes
from far away to touch us. Dying
or alive, we'd be touched.

That first night, caskets
opened at a trace
of the comet's tail. We saw graveyards
shift the angle of
their slopes as bodies, new dead
and old, rose
in single acts of upheaval.
The year the comet
crossed our sky, lilies closed,
evening and morning. We
burned candles hoping night
would bring in all its fears, this
one fear, to join us in the world.

We were not denied. Stars
went away, returned with weather.
Years of horse or dragon
turned and we grew timely, old as
animals we'd passed through.
If none of us would ever again see
the comet, we thought that
fitting. Once in our lives, afraid
for the world, for ourselves
and the life we'd made, we had
had our chance to be human.

A COMPASS FOR MY DAUGHTER

North is where the shadow
of the sky
retreats. North is a way back
to Grandfather, to night
animals we miss but are afraid
to befriend again.
You'll see long
clouds moving down someday. Remember
then, it will be time.

               Everywhere,
always, welcome the gift
of rain. Rain comes from where the streams
have gone. It is never
not at home. When you're sick, remember
the circle
of water, red message
at dusk. Look west: everything
returns.

      Southern luster
of feathers, the light in your skin.
The living turn there
and come to rest. Fire is its
color. Color is its real
name. Yellow
direction, warmest wind, the child
you once were.
South.

        Face east in your heart
and you'll begin
all journeys new. I bring you this far
so I can leave you. So I can tell you our bodies are clocks
and compasses—we have it in us
to know the time to
turn and point away.
Face east
in your heart and my leaving
signals return. Leaving is
all around us. Dying, too. Lives
move from room to room,
and they turn,
and they change
courses, drown, and are revived
at sea, on land,
in whatever air they breathe.

Your mother and I love you. You are
the beach. We are the next lonely wave.

MARCH DAY ON A NORTH COUNTY MARSH

—a pen-and-ink sketch by J. Dawson

Beyond the common dowitcher and whimbrel
lies a world comes to its end in wet air
alive over the marsh, in yards of tall
waves jarring the near beach. Birds dip for shrimp
all morning as if their beaks, half-submerged,
could read the secret life. An avocet
wades until its three colors double, startle
two birds apart. One flies like a soul

through water deeper than what is here.
And the teal, pipit, and rail wade—all fly
low over water clouded by tide,
nervous feet. There is plenty to live on,
enough to fear. Under the flooded sand,
a hundred wings practice the close of winter.

FAMOUS PERSONS WE HAVE KNOWN «««« 2000

LON CHANEY, JR., AT THE SUPERMARKET
IN CAPISTRANO BEACH

You'd see them now and then, on the fringe
of their stardom—Dick Van Dyke, for instance,
sober at last after his show dissolved.
Mostly they aged well, in chinos and golfer's tan,

not a mark out of the ordinary
except for the too-white teeth, or they carried
the torque of who they were and no longer were
in a kind of walking hammerlock—plain

Bob Denver eating steak in surgeon's garb
at the El Adobe. You'd wonder why
that woman in a fox stole walking her hound
could look at you once, all of 12 years old,

and convince you to be her grandson forever.
Did you recognize who cast the spells?
Would they someday reveal themselves
like the gray man behind you at checkout,

shuffling forward with all of us, quiet,
eyeing his eggs for cracks and counting his milk,
heaping bananas high against the night curse
of leg cramps? Just as the clerk turns our way,

he straightens up at the gum rack and growls,
paws half-raised and bared, and the eyes,
the terrible eyes wide and red and old
relaxing now into all our delight.

ROETHKE ON FILM

Huge as blowpipes on the ferry deck
drifting toward the bay, he stared through rain
and the bear-weight of muscle and blood
around his bones. There to the south grew clouds,
and the Olympics grew through them, through snow
to a heaven of the gods of speech.
Out of thick sky, their children had fallen
in names around him: Juan de Fuca,
Point No Point, Seattle. The world grew children of sound.

Of course he postured for the camera. Toady
cinematographers poured him drink
after drink and asked him to stand by the hearth
long hours after it roared. He should have
set their bags on fire, *then* recited.
He should have read Jane's elegy from a burning
house—saw then who would stay until the end.
Oh, I know who cared about image more than most.
Crossing the Sound, the cigarette hung just right.

Let water turn, root invade new ground, let
self assume its totem self—all clumsy
bear of it—and let Roethke be praised.
On a near hill inside us, leave his body
face-up in rain. Visit the corpse
as it grows away from its parts, a quiet
musical digression, stench to stench, blood
to bone to powder down a river warbling
toward salt, the map chorused with names.

SURFING ACCIDENT AT TRESTLES BEACH

When James Arness fractured his skull, my mom
took all the names and numbers, she

got the son's autograph, an X-ray tech
laying that cracked head down.

Sand in his hair turned up as tangled stars
awaiting diagnosis. All

around his brain on the light table,
a universe held, the victim

conscious now in the next room, cracking jokes,
asking for Doc and Kitty. He reached

for my mom, faked hallucination.
He offered to sign his wrecked board,

snapped in half and fluttering over tide pools.
By the time the on-call came,

he'd recited Yeats and Robert Service,
lost his balance once, invited

everyone to his house, took those loose words
back, ordered ten Shakey's pizzas

for the crew. Near as ever after that,
Dodge City boiled up once a week,

and I watched for the lawman's cracks to show.
Would he kiss Chester

or take a bribe? Would he turn to gardening?
Instead I saw him cut and slice

through kelp beds of violence, free-falling
wave-tip to base in pursuit

of the cruel. He guarded home and gold,
bright beach of our dream. And so

it came to pass that tropical storms
arrived regularly

in Kansas. Pier timber rattled straighter
than train or slug toward bent palms

inside the Longbranch Saloon. I was too
young to understand, but these were

the early days of metaphor. It was
the end of the West as I knew it.

MANSFACE

—*December. Green River, Wyoming*

Like Cathedral Rock or Newspaper Wall,
it's a stretch to see what's in the name. From south
or east of town, from north before driving
through the double tunnel under Castle Rock,
you see nothing but cliff rubble

with a Christmas tree at the crown. Then finally
from the west it's clear as ever, and not calm
like sculpted heroes in the Black Hills,
or praying, like accidental Indian
maidens on ledges every 20 miles

in mountain country. No, the rock there
places him in the middle of some agony,
his face turned 45° upward, the nose
and forehead bony or warted, the mouth
wide open as if that fossil Scrooge,

limed with trona, coal, and sandstone,
suffered the worst after only one bad dream.

Shoshoni called the river *Seeds-ke-dee*
but left the cliff unnamed. Trappers passed it.
From where he set out in love of stone wall
and water, John Wesley Powell
couldn't have ignored that face chin-pointing him

toward Flaming Gorge. On a walkway
above the UP tracks, it's not hard to see
my great-grandfather, yard master in 1912,
looking up every now and then to see
the light had changed, and the face and its color

with the light, the way we notice those things
out West, then turn back to our work.

Now the rock names a street, liquor store,
realty, rental warehouse, civic group, beauty
academy, the high school annual.
And so, after time, what we name
names us. From age 4 onward, children

put Mansface in every
drawing of town—make it, because they must,
less threatening, more and more like
grandfather taking his afternoon nap.
Students make up legends

for the visiting poet to praise
and take back home. Every April, Mansface
captures winter in its throat: You can hear
the ice breaking. Mansface hides the last wolf
in its ear: All summer it hears news

all the animals know. It learns the future. Even now,
it's talking to us, it's saying No to what's coming.

"TO MY VERY GOOD FRIEND, [SIGNED] JIMMY HOFFA"

—my grandfather's photograph

After we put you in ground, your dead boss
smiled a week on my mantel: a brief
interior grotesque. I never confessed
my friends thought you crooked because of him.
Even when they found you old, on your knees
in bird-of-paradise and rose, your hand
meant the feigning shadow of sin to them,
the shears even more proof, dirty with land

you probably didn't earn. Were my house
an American cathedral, his face
outdoors and stone, draining floods from high slate,
he'd belong in his weird way, steering worse
ghosts back to Hell. But I grant him this peace
and bury the look, these concrete shoes an old hate.

THE HIGH LAKE PAST THE FIELD

In the near-dawn moving across
blue flax and black, stitching near rocks
to gray rocking hillside, oak,

she gives herself back, atom by
atom, to her reassembly.
She reaches water and can walk.

Automatic as the amen of chard
gone rhubarb-red to seed, he again sits
and again feels for the easing of knots
he bound himself with without his knowing.
Amen to the small death strokes inside,
to their minority, to his more-than-
50-percent wanting to flourish
despite the strain easing more slowly now,

slow as whole days. On his knees in the garden,
he tears second-generation weeds from root
and willing earth. On the dark, unsure ground
where spirit grows its wheat, he kneels slowly
down. Stars do not come out inside the chest.
Work, love, song are the sound of the chemical
hoe and nighttime angel moving hill
to small spinach hill, preparing his yield.

Now that we're dying, on our way to fame
wider than our skins will stretch, you need to know
I saw the stones give birth to you
where that waterfall, far south of us now,
fell from prairie to ravine. I saw you
take shape from the mist, nothing for a heart
at first—no brains or ankles, no eye
or attitude—but then the hands came to life
and the body of you around them,
and even then the way you leaned against
a shore oak, touching it like a wound
you'd come out of the earth to heal, told me
everything. Who are we to keep magic
from leaking into our lives? Your hands
in their birdish way careened through the air
over a hundred rough men's homes. Women
loved you, too, Ana, and not just for the bread
which was the bread of laughing and dance
and life but for the sight of you
coming inside us, tilting on your wing,
the wind of your passing alive in our guts
like a courage we could never lose.
You were more real than we deserved.

Even as our dogs give out and the bear
makes its mile-wide circle until we drop,
I match you glide for glide. We're getting close
to that place on the ice we can lie down
head-to-head, two points of a star, the length of us
one compass mark, the heavens drawing

its slow rings above us as we die. I'll
save for then the story that makes us
rescuers of the world. You can tell me yours
as flags of every expedition
rip in bluster at the top of the world.
Submarines run softly through the dark
beneath our boots, voices coming up
through lines no different than time.
And this, this is where we've been heading
all along. We're walking square
into the bare music of living, Ana.
The miracle of your hand points the way.

MEDITATION

She must begin without discerning who lit
today's candle or why the rose-headed
finches haven't yet come to feed. Too long ago
rain stopped falling firm, without quarrel,

through the airscape of her spirit. Fenceboards
rattle in their slats inside this new rain
not trying to drop, not intending
to wash or ruin, to have watchers find in it

pain or the end of pain, navies of slugs
moving out from beneath the home, the fence,
the pile of rusting cans. The heart swivels back
while a nearby floor draws in elm-and-tractor song

from outdoors. She is a candle of sound,
a field uncontaminated by the known.

DOUGLAS ISLANDS

A hundred yards off Miller Point,
just north of the big island, I pull
the throttle all the way
back to a crawl. The dead wake lifts beneath

me, heading alone toward mid-lake, and I let
shiny tackle catch and drop
in that quick glide left over from the
race out of Table Bay.

Years ago you showed me
around those two acres of fir and berry.
Thirty years ago I got drunk
there the first time, swam nude off the

lake-facing shore, turned down dares to swim
to the small island, short
as your boat. I circle both, rock shelves falling,
rising, that one lure behind me

like the forgotten wish to keep
finding you in kokanee and char.

LAKE BOTTOM

Tying up at Goose Island, she dove in, angled
down and over the mossy shelf of
granite and fry to the dropoff. She swam
with mackinaw into greener and greener
shade, and the belly spots of Dolly Varden

drew her down, pink coals. When she reached bottom
she could hear the glacier
still grinding south. Moraine fell all
around her onto the deepest
char and bull trout, onto the lost

reel and just flickering spoon, aspen leaf, can,
onto the belt of the murder victim,
aluminum slide. It rained and rained more stone
inside that icy ghost, and she lay down
hearing fire under silt, saw then her hands

work magic with the dark: bringing salmon
to birth from a fingertip, scything
the choker weeds, turning rubble into
food. Far above, the boat she came in
slipped from its knot around a ponderosa. Drifting

for two days, it broke up at last on the state beach.

THE DOCK IN WINTER

spills itself out as the lake drops.
It gives up a lost wrench

from green moonslope already dry
by first snow. I walk

under ghost trails of perch
and the odd cutthroat. I make a circle

around all the shrinking beams.
I know I must drown this way,

over and over. I must die
and walk again, lean against the bone-white

crossbar watching the lake
freeze backward

into the Flathead and Lewis ranges,
all those mountains north into Glacier Park.

LOOKOUT ON MILLER POINT

We reached the top with scrabble
in our shoes, with blood on the palms
that gripped the willow, pulled each
other up those last ten yards. There

we could see our wheezing selves.
We sat on a rock ledge and breathed
east, Table Bay behind us
and down, two hundred feet. And there

again the two islands, and two
miles out to river current,
log, salmon, and weed,
and another five to the east shore.

Thirty miles north and south. South wind,
an osprey diving. I pointed out
the winter cougar den
and lichen. You saw flintrock,

then Canada, all fifty-three
years from London to L.A.,
thirty more to that Point, inches
between us. I hold you there now,

keep us from risking our necks
on the way down. I held you to stone
even as we skidded
toward Doc Patterson's drive, the dark

of the woods what we limped through
home, your game knee and muscles
tightening, my limp because of yours
and because I grew up with you.

SHRINKING

She gets up every day out of the ground
and garden rained on by her oldest grief,
her red-black tangle of petals so poison
they damage the eyes just to look. She

gets out of bed to find in the mirror
ribs and hips about to break out
of her skin, the face tight as a fist but
disappearing into eyes and the flat

mouth, everything shrinking like her small breasts
careless as waves of meringue, like her dark sex
where no one is ever allowed again.

On the phone at work, she chips at her mother
—*useless bitch, 80 years old and still*
got your head up your ass—chips until sparks
set fire to new abuse and ash

covers her desk like gray snow. She works it all
over and over into that soil
she comes back to, composting rage
and wreckage equally, the best of all

gardeners. There the last of her mother
restores the cineraria. Orchids
keep their heat all winter inside her,
even as the body pinches

its acid kingdom, shrinking like outer space
to her rescue or ruin, this weak sun
a kind of star she wants to live by.

THAT YEAR

The first tree, Chinese elm, made second base
and all the cheer of thousands, hovering high
and dark like shade. The first street ended dead
at the half circle of rhododendron.
You could smell the ocean ten miles away.
You could slide down the pitch of wild grass
to parking lot and grocery.

That year you first named evil, a man trolled
yard-to-yard for kids. A whole week, wildfire
spilled down the ridges, deer and puma stunned
by daylight neighborhoods. Evil found you,
a whisper in the loud skull. Ignored you
all through the rioting of August
worming its way toward a voice.

REDWING

When we decided the river was God
and the cave her ringing tune, we stooped
to every roll of stampede, to all gray storm.
When we decided the river meant us
harm, the voice in redwood darkened too,
an ear in the gut blown to sandstone.

When we forgot evil, we forgot ourselves.
Walkers doubled, tripled as they crossed
the mall, rain washing each from the other.
We owned every bone. At night someone screamed
from the hut. We drove on, carried away
by dead populations as if shoved by a wave,

the fumbling hooves of talk, as if we were
the last redwing straddling the bison's hump.

AFTER BEING QUIET FOR A LONG TIME

You'd let the tongue wait longer. The slick road
heart-to-lip grow dangerous with weeds.
You'd stand at the open door watching earth
close a snowy mouth over each word.

A bell choir changed you. Squirrels in the attic.
The crying girl. A pencil breaking.
Where does all the noise go, going inside?
Waves slap and flatten on a cold lake.

After being quiet for a long time, you'd slip
over yourself toward talk, not at all
like you thought. You'd fall through anger and lust
as bad as always, the road without toll,

no bridges locked from here to either coast.
Someday again you'd think yourself through a meal,
biting through to silence. Quiet through dishes,
through sex or shower. Quiet through asking

or asking forgiveness. The larch, a dock,
your small boat would wait for you like the lake
for the first oar-pull into the middle,
for a word to say without breaking.

MOON IN SMOKE, TETON PARK

We waited until you carved
the yellow darkness out, moved

land away like one still loved
but a burden—pulling up

in light you owned, did not own,
as wind exploded, as green

flared to red in praise of you,
circling, bringing back the dark seed.

DEMONSTRATION

I never told you about Tonopah,
100° into the Mojave, the Mizpah Hotel
my grandfather and I stayed at
blurring in red-brick waves, the slot machines
clutching and rolling. I knew Boron,
town of the dead coyote, lay up the road.
I knew I'd have my last meal there
before crawling lower than sage, just above snakes
toward the flat basin and the one plywood shack
trimmed with single-rod antennas.
I never told you I was there when circles flew outward
on the sand, when that shack sunk ten feet
into desert floor, a huge cake suddenly collapsed.
I never told you I lay on my stomach
at the edge of the explosion,
swimming in shock waves, riding a roar
still traveling in every direction of space.
When I saw the shack disappear, when I saw bolts
of lighting ground-to-cloud and, sideways,
hill-to-hill, I knew I could never
look right at you again, nor even Pop
in his room back in town 30 years before.
In our home 1000 miles east, you were teaching
our youngest to talk. I drove back to you
on the other side of speech,
practicing a way to blow memory back together,
rehearsing the way to meet your eyes
without our skulls showing.

THE LUNAR DRIVER

Sage connects to lava rock mile by mile.
West of Atomic City, blue flowers
in the craters of the moon. Jackrabbits
now where the sheep kill was. Road following
wind. Handsful of grass. The blue wind. The black.

Lyndon Johnson stood here for the roadside
plaque, Arco still in flames. The Big Lost
and Little Lost rivers disappeared into
their own sinks, ten miles apart, at the Idaho
National Lab. And thousands come home

to their roads like clouds. And any given
dead one, bird or girl, might circle this place
missing life, backing off the plateau
into sky, letting go of one green wheel.

BREAD

The day we heard about her cancer,
the kind in the brain and lungs, whatever that means,
the longest cold spell of winter slipped
away like short-term memory, now to the surface
and quietly over a set of falls, down
to a river silent and out of view. Each warmer day
dazed us with sun: My wife shoveled her walk
five doors west, I made them potato rolls,
and among women a chain of prayer
extended all over town. Looking for my friend,
I wanted to touch him on the shoulder, that gateway
to another grief, just to ask what
he needed. I thought only of that exchange,
what I would say not to fumble, and I guessed
his jaded, grateful answer. I guessed
the humor there.

                     But it never worked that way:
Both of them simply disappeared
into the shrinking of tumors,
into managing pain, that escape in slow drives
between city and town that took them
by cow fields, brick barns,
any reminder of France. She was cold and hot
all at once those days, so they'd fidget
with the fan all the way back from the doctor's,
tires on wet road like bacon sizzling, my friend
asleep a lot of the time. When they talked
it was not like in the movies. I now know
this all third-hand, and what you need to understand

is that in two months she went
from fear to desire, he from fear to love.
They let go into loneliness knowing
it part of the orbit.

                    I only found this out
later. What I did those months was find signs
everywhere: in the weather, the start of Lent,
my cough, every gesture of hers
before I'd heard, the air, the soil.
On Ash Wednesday evening, the church was her body
we lived and sang to fill. Black pressed
the stain out of glass. I ate
and drank from her, our mutual sacrifice.
There are times in your life when you feel
inside great unspeakable mystery.
It makes you tremble. That is the sign.
There are other times, growing your own grief,
when you force an utter
sense on the world. I never cared for her
the way I thought I did. She left my galaxy,
my river with its talking stones. Am I
unkind to say this? I am. I talk
like someone who will die alone.

I don't really know desire, or love, the roles
for leavers and stayers. Every time
that lake comes back in memory, though,
the ice long gone, the sun high, hot,
salmon biting at any color or flash,
the world composes itself exponentially
around the meal appearing as I say it

on picnic tables at the end of this
great day. Everyone I've ever cared for
is here. We complain about the hornets.
We wonder about the cold breeze out of Canada.
And all of us praise the fish, the whole spread
two grandparents made because feeding
the hungry is what it's always all about. No one
has died yet, although I know they will.
They are feeding us, even as they leave.
They are inside of us, kneeling and singing.
They break us and tear from within
as if we were bread. They help us
turn new into the life we didn't know was already here.

THE UNTESTED HAND «««« 2008

FOURTH-PERSON SINGULAR

There came a way to drive the map
of the blood vessel, and to nudge
cynicism right through the cool

aquifer, into the trusting
well. It took centuries to fail
and to win. It took four wrecked

deserts west of here, all the tar,
your dying human God, dead hawks,
clouds alive with an unreal heat.

It took the loss, stumbling forward
after the end of books and walks
to the store. We recognized our

new selves in that way the oldest
ones, bent to drink shining water,
greeted the beginning of the

world. Everyone used the new names
after that. They reached low into
the body, fearing and joyful,

and out came this way of walking,
flying, and drowning all at once
in a voice cousin and human.

Leafy, wet, growling, high-pitched, rude,
it talks in us from under tide
lines, the untested hand pushing

up and out.

THE STARS IN MONTANA

At Hebgen Lake at 3:00 A.M., the dog
blew out our tent and chased the other one whose barking,
all night, came in short bursts jerked south by wind.
I hadn't slept anyway, thinking of the quake

upriver in the 50s, all those campers
under a rock slide now, under water.
I lay still as my wife got our dog,
came back, and invited me outside

to look at stars. She still remembers the flood of them
low, tight above that narrow valley, waves
slapping in dark, the stunted wheezing
firs of the campground, a cold green table,

my staying in the bag. They were heavens
we could have easily shared, but didn't.
I still remember the waking dream,
its temporary paralysis, each

bark whisked away, the meadowlark's flute
when morning finally came. We stayed married
all the way west to Twin Bridges, to Bannack,
to the ground where Chief Joseph quit and fought

no more forever. It was the last trip
we took without plan or children, those stars
we followed later into thinner sky
awash with half-orbits and resentments, that awful

joyous flood of heart and weak place.

CURSING THE ORACLE

You came from over the hill when ocean
we know about now trickled slow as first
wind on a dream. On porches, on long swings
in yards, you saw ahead that whale-jammed valley
north of our tower, heard the clapping rock
and clam as wave upon wave broke through larch.
You showed mothers where they'd snag in kelp beds.
You showed the old man where, just weeks ago,
fog rolling through our town, you'd shine his stone.

We swam here that day. Salt dried us out
that last afternoon of real sun. We heard the roar
with minutes to spare, but it was madrigal,
our hushed blood loving the tide and alarmist
gulls. As west closed down on us, we forgot
the life before drowning, its matchbooks
and apple cake, a woman's forearm, her eye
looking back. I forgot my stammering boy.

Who are you now to recall me to survivors?
I rolled once in a green-dark foam and died
long before the echo reached you. In months
of rain and wind, I scattered myself
on your visions. You wear my salmon-robe, my
lightning strikes you. The ocean came to me,
and it swallowed me up. You know nothing.

PRAYER

In the thick basement I never found
years ago in Los Angeles, ground hums
like all the voices I've ever heard,
all the wind, the train wreck, the other

accidents. While my son's feet make their
thunder on flooring above me, I reach
back to those ears and eyes I was. Scared
half the time for breath, before that for spirits

in air who would take it away,
somehow the cross of a crow's flight and mine
would wake me, and once I grew happy
at the blurred touch of red Os freckling

Loch Levens. Gusts came down the draw then whipping
cottonwood and stiff sage. The canyon babbled
toward its valley like the stream. That hot day
my grandfather and I hiked three miles

around rattlers, boulders huge as rooms, for fish,
and I knew I'd be afraid a lot if I
ever grew up, if the world didn't kill me.
I thought of the slaughtered Packard, decades upside-

down and rusted by the snow-cold stream,
I thought of the jackrabbit in those last
seconds after a hawk shadow darkened
its path. And once I grew happy,

a non-sequitur, wet stones bending water
into speech, into words too difficult
to say and so left unsaid—there in that wild
air over the stream, here in this unsure

basement where earth stays quiet
while it remembers everything.
                                        Lord,
when I lose my voice, make of me the moment
when flickering leaves, a wind-driven

heat, and the trout—set on its last hook
and running—are one. Let the fish pain
come in. Make of me the molecules of pain,
blown sand, breathing rocks, cloud. I will praise you.

CRACK BABY ON TV

In old stories, you wouldn't die.
Born with a wrenched leg, with eyes open, marked
by God to fill out the curse with skin and bone,
they'd take you to a wild place, wolves yowling,

set you down on straw next to stone,
cold coming on, and you'd lie there quiet,
the king's man walking away and night falling,
each star defender—then the shepherd came.

Now you're the dénouement in knots
of wire and tube. Your heart rings hourly. You're
all atwitter when the green one lifts
and rocks and rocks under the hard white trying

to still this rattle and jerk. If you knew
snow, it would be floating down. If an island
the size of a needle hole in the Pacific,
it would be here, warm, holding only you.

Instead, cameras flash moment to moment
in your eyes, and white blows up inside
like tiny bombs. We find you on the news
next to other wars, and we see clearly

as parents through the glass each beautiful line,
each sure signal of genius waiting
to rescue our city from its plague. You'd rule
years in glory, marry high, then fall

like any hero once the final maimed
glimpse of you turned back into ourselves.

SMALL SONG

Something in you squeezes the eye blind.
It takes and takes, and when the mind and her eye
close on the fish, the dazzle on
aluminum, the spiritless thumb in you

presses out light easily as ants going home
single-file. It's a grim joke, that hand
sweeping in and out of the visible.
So direct its guard of dark

the hundred diplomats in you can't guess
yet how to talk to it. A black flag
whips high and unafraid in the close
altitude of blood. The world would have you

throw the ocean's green there, the mad
but living cackle of nutcracker, all
you could absorb, but you've been too long
player of the black anthem, the small song

playing out despair in everyone,
tempting us to feed it, to give it feet
to walk and hands to clap shut at the
recognition of any simple thing

we could believe in.

THE EAST SHORE

Across gray lake, cherry orchards load up
sky and woods with smudge high as the Swan Range
behind them. We know frost breaks the leaves off
in ourselves, and we know fall blows the oldest

new wind to a bald man, still with that half-grown
voice, living in our dimmed homes. But cold
we don't argue with: Across the face
of a lake urging trout more and more

into the slow-turning thought of itself,
grove owners burn what they have watched, branches
old as themselves or their daughters,
limbs wind-ripped or sawn. Well past our own yield,

we ease toward the invisible, burning ourselves
quiet. We change again to quick-rising ash.

YOU FELT HAPPY

As its water formed a low dome
above the level of this cup,

you walked through that light air brimming,
watching your joy on its brink of

spilling over, and you asked if
a weight had gone, or if these ties

knotting your walk to elm and dead
river, to the gutter-sleeping

and mall-haunting, had suddenly
snapped. You floated, that smile inside

your face and budding at the mouth's
corners, the wind an envelope.

You glided through noon as if through
all the hexagrams of change, sticks

beating above you still on their
trees, rocks clapping through frost and mud

toward light and quiet thunder's end,
weather scissoring around each

edge of grass, lip, or complacence,
each excess of hope, or of doubt.

FIN DE SIÈCLE SONNET OUT OF TOWN

—Wendover, Utah

Across the salt flat, white-hot and miles wide,
hills cut the surface like black fins. Roads end there
if you believe your eyes. Gulls trade in their
first and only question, hovering, for that high
circle of mockery, what birds must have cried,
until Mormons came to stay, when sickened herds
gave out, when ox carts overturned
and the westward passage died, all those eyes

left here for pecking. Meanwhile, the wavy
highway, black as a stalled car or hill,
disappears in basalt. Where would the century
have me go? Not back. Not west. Nowhere still
ground zero, the earth all glass. Nowhere leaves
don't shade the grosbeak, don't wrinkle on the sill.

TOWARD MANKATO

As we headed east from the mountains
that north-south compass
melted into its directions, then everywhere,
everywhere was center, the needle
confused without granite.

Prairie birds came in all color,
low to the ground, bunting
by blue bunting, flicker after jay. Sky bent
and raced away like sky in Los Angeles,
1953, it all beginning again.

At night we dreamed crickets
rose and fell on wires of sound. A snake
breathed shallow under cool roots.
We sailed through new air
between the emptying

Platte and Arkansas, hearing the cranes,
hearing the dying hidden
in long grass, a new song riding
the changing waves of grain.
We had begun again. Thirty years later,

the voice we used our first
months alive came back like mild screams
not warning us, not omens, but weaving
the fabric of each prairie night.
We were the sound of insects and wind,

last broken neck of Dakota
120 years before, that day white
and everyone in dark
to watch the end of Indian war. Snow jumped up
from the street like minor argument

against any single death.

JULY

In hated towns, even, churches ring
their morning bells—at eight or nine, maybe.
In summer, when a breeze floats the last of night-cool
north, bells ring on that same breeze,
reminding the most hateful banker,
walking to work, of the farm
he grew up on, three fields away from the Methodist
chapel, and even a budding thug,
en route to slashing Harold Nystrom's
favorite hybrid rose, will notice a twinge
the first knelling makes
in his rib. His job is not to remember it.

Then musical air turns normal.
Any town continues to pay its bills and have its
accidents, while the nearly clean river
eats a slow way through the concrete floodwall.
Day will heat up. Something memorable
may or may not happen during the lunchtime
hustle: people have their seizures then,
or get engaged. Either way,
afternoon will begin to crawl
beneath its humidity, the black locust more
tropical-looking, passing trucks
more and more like the tireless engines

of wilt and misery. Just before six,
businesses all closed, most people home
or playing softball, leaves will start
a new trembling. The coals

will almost be gray enough for the meat.
Reading the paper outdoors, one person will feel
cool. For a moment, tricycle sound will stop.
Bells will have started ringing again,
a kind of slow-moving front
gone after their minute, raining on both
the beautiful and the damned,
drenching everyone with sure, unexpected music.

YARD

1

Clouds full of ocean blown back, partial vines
tapping light as fingers on the trellis,
wind fills the yard. Wind—and with clear sky now,
grass frozen green in January sun,

the matter of history we resent
having to think about. While life goes on
under compost, under patio slab, my father's
face composes in the forest, the one

on that hillside beyond the twenty thousand
homes—there, the farthest hill today. We
forgive ourselves not hate, but nothing, not
too little love, but none of it, as a yard,

swaying like the photo of a yard I
never lived in, still holds onto its edge,
hawthorns whipping.
                    If the unloving hand
arrives at itself in filling the birdhouse

with seed, then so be it. And amen, alder
split and stacked, split again some winter day
like this one: frost on bark, glare on inner
wood, spark at the place where axe blade and wood

and sun and force of the faraway arms
come to meet.

2

        Why am I divided
like the yard? Its beaten fences keep
two neighbors' stares out, but not their moths
or arguments, not autumn leaf-smoke. Am I
like the back jumble of stake and board, leaning,
almost prostrate, over—foreground to the field
it's giving in to? If I fall or bend
enough, do I become the pasture
of blackberry and horses?

                And why, like the yard,
partly this, that, am I separate
from myself? Even garden stubble, rich
in dying, feeds the chickens if they're let out.
Even ash mounds in those dark, unused caves
of hedge feed something else, are fed
by the wheelbarrows from elsewhere. Wind
fills this yard, but everything, everything
bound by its frost, stays put.

3

                                Over the grounds
and fountains of our wealthy heroes, the same
juncoes fly like orphan items of the self.
Flight lines whisper jacaranda to elm,

small spring to bank of trout pond, above
and touching every kind of lawn. If yards
copy lives, we don't begrudge the rich their various
souls. Juncoes return as to the scene

of an accident that made them alone,
and there, in the broad acreage under handsful
of birds, we learn not to envy the complex
inner fates of those we make sport of

hating, or of the unpropertied insane,
rich with fates of similar, landless anguish.
We can be simple. In my ten-dollar
chair left out since August, I am crisscrossed

by shadows and the real, invisible
lines floating down. The orphan-master is in.

4

Like clouds that moved back, we hold fast, raining,
raining first ice, then gray and green on the counties
of a room, blown through the whole house, warmer
now, melting chilled furniture, washing clean
the mirrors. Outside, the two systems join. I
rain on the rain that falls on me. The yard,

under both of us, pushes its winter
stones toward light. What comes back ties my hands
to the work at apple tree or woodpile,
my feet to the unmarked path from iris
to lily bed. House, yard, worm, stones pushing toward
light, flicker, horse, pasture, millrace, hill where

orphan birds turn cloud—I knew them all
before they rose from lawn, headed for the breathless spaces.

WESTWARD EXPANSION

You get someplace and stay
and don't get your ass
kicked soon enough. Begin
to think you own the view

and water. Then the cut
wire, wildfires at the edge
of acreage. Even
rocks know, playing out their

last gold, that your time
is through, the new screaming
goshawk means poverty
just like before, but in

new clothes: it's never
going to be about land
again. Bleeding to all
four skies, all flags blowing

in their winds, it's never
about land when you look
for a way back to center.
Here on the horizon

your feet touch, you're too rich
still to know. You can't do
a thing but home in on it
crossing and re-crossing

this hidden continent.

STORY COMING BACK

In the last years before the hills
grew homes, stilts and picture
windows gold at sunset, the Pacific
crashing at the sand as the dream
came true, we ran along these cliffs,
up each side, our blood
drumming the skins of our faces, along
ridges yellow with wild grass,
perforated with retreating mice, snakes,
each bird in the updraft
mum in its backing away, loud
in its low, rifle-shot escape.

We thought nothing, running,
of men getting rich on the air
and ocean sound, the orange sunlight
we ran through. We thought nothing of
our feet delivering their messages, of the story
coming back which was a history of waves
higher than those clouds, the ground
unsettled over and over, the birds
transient as climate, wind confused by
ice and fire, its own past.
We thought nothing, running,
of ourselves extinct in that scene
as our blood, later, pounded us
further away from home, that field
miles from papers beginning
and ending the shuffled battle,
miles we would learn to rely on later,
the hills covered, running from our blood.

And we live here now. And we run through the
quiet park and down to the living
pools at low tide, the red
all around us settling toward dusk
as we plan the murders of rich men
and what has failed in ourselves since the open
land, murders we will never commit
for the crime of forgetting one's joy,
for loving the force that hoards the poor
man's craft. We run,
healthy as the enemy pocketing the key
that jails Hector Márquez, both of us
thirty today, our sons
days away from being born.

TERROR IN THE DESERT

All the thought that hot day came to waiting
for the lake to break through the dam's high face
like a peony, then like mad water,
out a man-made wound. The ridgetops baked.
Here and there the green flags of eco-warriors.
There the press. There the angry Army Corps
behind the yellow crime-scene tape, its view
better than anyone's. Experts at delay,

the buzzards loomed. Brown towhees scratched the sand.
The blast each heard was just a sonic boom,
a mock-war eight miles up, an argument
the ear makes with the eye. When the quiet blast
comes, our eyes hurry toward it—lovers, victims—
that violence ours, each boat calm down its noisy chute.

THE WHALE

July storm: bullets of rain, clearing
wind. Unloving men and women
walk their crisscrossing ways, marking the X
where heat turned invisible and failed.

The weekend city fills with missed
chances while the roadbed flowers. Finches,
pigeons work their one fallible song,
rooting-on the prophesied death of commerce.

Traffic lines stay put. Chinese elms watch over their
sidewalk inheritances of earth. Underground,
dark stones shift, begin rolling, sparking
as they roll, and two great fins

ripple in that slow, heavy motion black
as the whale turning, pipe and cable straining.

THE OWENS VALLEY

In *Chinatown* it was where water
came from, where a flume, side-saddled to hill,
rode south to L.A. and often blew up.
My grandfather remembered bought-out, angry
farmers going dry, and the rioting
at a far city hall. Thirty years then,
long past a wet Easter, and two ranges
drained toward the car, that smooth lake bed
we passed on the way north to Rock Creek.

In 1960 we read the plaque
at Manzanar, ducked in and out of the stone
sentry house guarding nothing then or now.
We never found the town layout in sand,
but I know it from Adams' photographs.
I saw faces, a church and garden. Last year
I broke onto Water and Power land
to find any trace of tin or cinder block
in 103° heat under Mt. Whitney.

At the top of the valley, cabin and creek
were still there, the loud rush of trout.
The same log and rock got me across
at each same point, the same cottonwood
hissing. I fished the water north
into steep, thinning gorge, a mile past
anything familiar. Then I saw in shade
the puma, not thirty feet away. I spilled
back to camp. I took those eyes away with me

on my own ride south between sierra
and sierra, past Little Lake,
where I once hunted pheasant and nearly
shot a dog, past China Lake, dry,
where the Navy tests weapons. Over the hills
south into L.A., the basin spread out
all its green and remembered names,
one of them mine, a place my son will ask about
casually, taking his small drink of me.

EVENING NEWS

After I jumped in the screen and began marching,
shook my fist in Lafayette Park,
built my tent, I looked back at you through the lens
touching the rest of the world.

I chained myself to a fence and the eloquent
sign. I was famous for a thin moment
as the camera panned us all, and I saw you
at home, surrounded by consequences

we had little time for. Juncoes
dodged your picture window, diving
into mile-wide woods. Indoors, you nodded
back at me, and a storm came ashore

across the whole country, and the power
failed. I drank left-handed without you, chains
clinking, thermos near empty, the ocean coming down
across the whole land hunting for its candles.

RADIOACTIVE CITY «««« 2009

THE ODDS

Finally, it turns out, he was against everything.
Against six-year-olds with baseball gloves
and red caps, against Jack Russell terriers,
Mustangs, Beetles, against chocolates after
dinner, three-hour movies, against movies
without plot or their bastard cousin, Film.

He marched against terror in Asia
and chained himself to the White House fence. He
wrote essays against polluted thought. He
practiced body painting like Farrah Fawcett,
all to oppose losing one's mind in public.

He fought pasta at every meal. He fought
cloves in ham. He fought the shrinking size
of ice cream tubs. He'd slice off an ear
if Pee Wee Herman would just stay off the news.

He was against taxes, big government, no
government, any manner of clown
from dog-catcher to Secretary of Defense,
against voting except to vote against, against
freedom, tyranny, against love.

He'd never been damaged as a child.
If he had, he'd still be against therapy. He was,
against his own best judgment, against
himself. Who could trust anyone so close?

Long ago he'd decided: He who was not
with him, was against him. He was against
most everyone. He did not kick against
the pricks, but that didn't mean he was for them.
He was against factory farming, animal testing,
GMOs, the WTO, bow-hunting
the deer in Rasmussen Woods, gill-nets, whaling,
seal hunts, against wearing fur, against
leather, against meat, against Coke, Nestle,
and Honeywell, against every
smart-ass, Indian-tobacco-smoking
vegan wearing petrochemical fleece.

He was even against walking. On the trail
by his house, deep in an oak savannah,
he growled at the smallest rodents and cursed
the cardinal's cheap tune. He was equally
against poison ivy and grass. If a bald eagle
swooped on him, he would argue
with its feathers. He was against the voice of God
in the creek, the constant nagging of angels
to go deeper into wild. His feet took him
places he would never believe in. They were
compass needles answering a greater
pull. He was against the North and South poles.

He was against the fascist years of Pound,
the suicide of Plath, the dissipation
of Dylan Thomas and Jackson Pollack,
John Cage's silence, the dead weight of
Soviet Realism, New Criticism, post-
and neo-Modernism, against

the hegemony of text, against the pimps
of dark art and self-immolation. Against
beauty, he made the poem that rebuked them.

He was against the vowel shift and most
contractions. He was against lemon zesters,
calamari, the execution of
Mata Hari, Harry Potter, fizzy
water, laughter, Daffy Duck, Chuck Norris,
Doris Day singing anything related
to Christmas, Miss Manners, Ann Landers, Gander
Mountain, Rin Tin Tin, cheap rhyme, your mother.

He was against the sun coming up and going down,
or rather, the earth turning. Or rather,
the way time gets into the act. Or rather,
the idea of history like too much loose
change in a threadbare pocket. Or rather,
your mother, who sold us all
downriver in 1862.

He was against everything, finally.
Even the patience of his wife, who really
should have kicked his ass. Even his dog,
who continued to snuggle his shoe. Even
the forgiving mirror, the soft couch
of his living room. Against even
John Coltrane, God bless him. Against even blessing.

What would it take to love something again?
A dream of thunder and lightning, a newborn
looking up into his eyes? He'd be

against that, too, rocking and rocking
his little package, the neighborhood
speeding by outside the window. Given
their odds, given the little song he keeps
the baby quiet with, he'd bet against it.

IN MANHATTAN, THE ORACLES DO NOT LIE TO HIM

This time, the face of the Blessed Virgin
staring up from a folded matchbook, four
draws to a poker hand studding her cardboard
gown, the fifth card hidden inside with all
her fire, a two of clubs, and down her back
an ad for business school, 1-800-
A-NEW-YOU. He doesn't even smoke, a mistake

he sat at that table in the first place. Still,
shimmering incidents track him in the park
like the eyes in haunted houses: A bunting
talks to him in code, *sweet-sweet, chew-chew,*
spit. The bench's grime scrawls fluent
Mandarin along the back of the sniveling man,
his hand out even in sleep. By the time

he reaches the great lawn, he's grown comfortable
at the center of meaning, the crux
of the mandala. He wonders if giant
monks drizzle sand on the city at night,
if Navajo *brujos* spin history
out of a hidden cave in Arizona. Who's
responsible, he wants to know and thank,

for the lamb shawarma at Mamoun's
in the Village? He wants to know who pulled
the trigger on the train that very morning:
whose hand, whose hand in the sky, whose hand
above the hand? Someone in orbit could look down
on one and all and see nothing, or trace
the golden hemline of the Buddha. All around him,

boys and girls play softball, football, then, farther away,
lacrosse until the lawn runs out and forest
begins. How do children, metaphors for humans
they never become, steady themselves
so easily on the limber blades of grass and walks
slick with fallen leaves and wayward spray
from fountains? How do bunting and jay

and squirrel, metaphors for motion and heart,
put up with each question and still
find their way? On a gray rock inside
the green woods, the man in a tuxedo
sings Italian to the secretive
rodent, the feral cat, all the uncatalogued
night species, the budding virus and bacterium,

each of them waiting for its colored
grain of sand. No one chases him toward
the tenor. Still, he's moving in that direction,
a wrinkle on the great lawn, a pixel
on the cornea of hovering, dispassionate
earthmakers, a blip on cave radar. He
thinks he knows this song the way he knew

a coat he once stepped into and drove
a car inside to another country.
He drank the local beer and listened
to its one river. He sampled
the national dish. When he returned, he never
noticed how his talk had changed—all his friends
swore to it—or how the animals

looked back at him when he whistled
the familiar tune out his door, under
his breath on the subway, past that holy
ashtray, the newsstand of doubt, past pilgrims
colliding with their grief, making his own
invisible trail to the center, long past the time
he hung that old skin back in his closet.

THEIR HERO STRAPPED TO HIS CHAIR
AT THE ALTAR OF FORSAKEN MALADIES

Praise after praise, they weigh him down,
each cure, each aversion of doom
there in his lap, his to claim,
and they all keep shuffling forward
to the mike, telling a story
of the savior with his name

who, touching them, dissolved the crutch,
who, speaking to them, rinsed the crust
from eye and heart, who alone
set angels inside them dancing
to one great tune, never asking
for a thing, thanks or honor.

He sinks into earth now, head bowed,
razors, canes, and manifestos
heaped on, around him. And sky
presses down, having its quiet way
with human triumph, these places
having their way with sacrifice.

AND SO IT CAME TO PASS

He raised goats and lived at the tree line,
sat zazen so he could count to nine
again. At sea level, grown-up humans
wrote letters to the leader or pined

for love. They fell into their children
or followed the money, as they'd been
told. On the sidewalk, an old woman burned
her scarf and hat for the last time, then

rolled her barrel to the next street. Planes
angled over rooftops on their way
to oil. *We're making progress,* the leader
was saying. *We have re-made the path*

to beauty. The mountain crumbled
if he let it, if he rang the small
bell of attention, counting past ten. Steep
cliffs flat as a plate, the war dulled

like a knife. A girl looked at the sky
as the giant weather of history
blew over, through her. She saw below cloud
the one bright light: his candle, her star.

FLATHEAD LAKE

1. Soundtrack

Before a salmon even breaks
the surface, a round sky will cave
in, a ring of mountain shrink
to the size of his slow reeling,
his whispered soundtrack, each feeling
its way along with every

rally and lull at the end of
the line. *Just say its name, real soft,*
his grandfather would say. *Some*
of the lake is swimming up to
meet you, darkness to daylight to
quiet, a word for each motion.

2. Short Sacred Journeys, Where and Why

To Miller Point. To the orchard
next to woods. To the stacked lumber,
the machine shop, the steady
dock. To the shallow place before
the drop-off. To two islands near
enough and always empty.

Compass points collapse. New cherries
hang in deep shade. Outboard and mice
make a common noise. Water
holds him up. He sees into dark
where char and salmon swim. He marks,
stroke by stroke, a path to the altar.

3. Passing Through

Every stay begins, night falling
or day falling, with the cold clean
paddle strokes to Painted Rock,
where someone 900 years gone
laid the thin marks, the red bison
down, left ravens to their talk.

Every stay ends, when day falls, night
falls, with the wild staring eye
he left there, taking strangers in
through fill and drain, come and go, eye
the rock could not let close fifty
generations past the man.

TURNING 50 IN MISSOULA

—in memory of James Welch

I always wondered how we'd land if sky
let go crossing the Continental Divide,
down through turncoat thermals, an engine
flaming, a wing-tip shorn, toward that cabin

next to the hay field next to the trout-jammed
stream. I always believed the smallest place
could save us, even as we screamed through space
at the clearing our lives would always owe

our lives to. Prairie lay forever east.
Ahead, the wide valley fretted out of reach.
Here we fell in between, time running out,
clipping the crowns of larch, a whole town

waving wide-eyed when our shadow marked them.
After skid and tumble, then the real gift.

ANGEL

The flat land chased the mountain from him,
nutcracker and smell of pitch, the hymn
a creek makes over stone old as the moon.
He learned to see level, to speak plain

as ivy against glass, these buildings
humming, on fire in their way, misery
the tuning fork for greed or any firm
hand wanting to reach down. He'd left that day—

left God whispering, alone—for clay,
for unreckoned air, the random flight
of birds, wave that would find him at the sea
lifting its dead, breaking his body.

AT THE END OF WINTER, HE KEEPS TO TRAVEL PLANS DESPITE A TERROR ALERT

He had left the moon behind,
a slim train lugging its light,
a castle of cheese, a horse
he rode once, falling in black.

He had left the moon behind
like a dime in the slot, pouting.
He left messages no one
would answer until oceans

tilted, crooning lunar night
on mute. He saw the rock then,
the one they brought back in bags
marked for the aerospace

museum. He saw that scuff
the astronaut's claw had made,
a place where the brush pushed back
a layer of dust he could

only call the moon's last breath.
Beyond that gallery, grass
lit up, and the Capitol
shone like a maniac's tooth.

People prayed everywhere to
black marble, to the obelisk.
Still, children rolled eggs across
the endless lawn, their one true flag.

PAPERWEIGHT

He left that tiny island with the stone
not knowing its daily weight on his mail,
an asteroid among earth's obligations,
held all that ever could be saved: the soul

flown pocket to pocket for years each time
he changed his clothes, soul like a jagged coin
singing with keys, shredding the thin lining,
soul at last on the desk where, unmoving,

the damage finally stopped. All around us,
homes collapse to lumber, dust. It's normal,
not wanting to die. To hold the planet
in its place. To stop the death song, joyful

as we fall into who we must be, our
atmosphere breached, the sea clutching a star.

He steps down from the wall where he's been dead
for three years, brown brick wall of a warehouse
high above streetball games and alley thefts,
a mother calling, a daughter shouting

back, wall where they play the movie of him
playing son at a kitchen nook, the dad
fighting over something dumb, the husband
swimming slow on top of her, his breath at

her neck, his tongue at a nipple. He steps
down to the last elm left in town. He won't
stop the thugs from baring their knives. He steps
through belief and onto the angled road,

danger a rule the others made for him,
this dizziness a spell death would not permit.

BAPTISMAL FONT

He leaned over the bowl
only to see his own face

looking back, and the ceiling
behind him, and the nothing

behind the hidden sky. Why

would he think this tiny sea
wasn't enough? The ripple,

the pin-sized holes in limestone
made from billion-year-old air.

AT 2:00 A.M.

In black, when he settles under
the sheets, his wife already hours
inside a lonely comma,
he listens for his son beyond
the wall, the padding feet, the knob
turning, the creaking stair down

to the sunlight dark of the den,
out to the porch, cigarette red
under stars, the boy's back flush
to the wood bench as on other
nights—as on another night, heart
blinking on, off from its tower.

ORBIT

His house, small as a circle of toys,
grew wider finally than the hemisphere,
taller than the last moon.

His boys had left long ago: Bill to
a wife, Carl to the radioactive
city. He counted quiet

each morning as if love had number
and the sound of every language painted
new colors on his wall.

His house, after all, sucked each thing in,
a huge lung, and he was the heart muscle
just under the tissue,

beating through the scream from another
continent's jail, an earthquake rippling north
to match his own clear pulse,

beating through the desert orphan's knock,
her stomach a small globe, the dust and flies
in orbit around it.

THE MISSING MAN

Chained in his cave, he knew to speak
to each hallucination, to
every father, flower, bell.

Even later, the angel found him
at his daylight address, asking
directions to the mouth.

NAMING EVIL

Could he if it split the elm in two,
if it swelled the ditch, the word bore through
to the heart of the matter: his daughter
asleep all winter under the snow.

Could he if his hand began to burn.
Could he if its eyes took their glass turn
toward vacancy and damage. Everywhere
the crows explode from their tiny room.

Could he if he knew he shared the air,
the footstep to a muddy edge, hair
limp around her face. Could he if he saw
how soft she was laid down, how it cared

almost, ditch weed a kind of palace,
the whole gray sky coming down, its face
a thing he knew from back home, fast water
knuckling over rocks, held to their place.

FALL

Like the sloth I would be looking
up toward the tree crowns, even though
I hung heavy from the longest branch,
all my weight supported by claws

and the stupid faith of these arms
moving me relentlessly toward
the outer reaches, the sweet new leaf
close to the place where I decide

when effort and desire will part.
The truth is, I don't want a thing
from this world. I look into sky
to flush out the cluttered detail

right in front of me. These ants,
for instance: They march onto my tongue
as if sinners could go somewhere
wet and dark with their grief, as if

I could release them easy
as a syllable. Who am I
to be a palace of expectation?
I'd rather fall to the new life.

ENTERING WYOMING

Without a name
for grass, he crosses

the invisible line
where the North Platte

narrows west,
where antelope hang

Walt Whitman
by his barbed-wire beard.

SCENE FROM A 1948 MOVIE

The boy with green hair runs across lawns,
climbs the sharp fence until the dark
opens up and he is stumbling through woods
like Frankenstein escaping the mob,

children he knew once coming his way
with taunts and scissors, the fear of his
hair in their eyes like small torches lighting
the forest path, setting his whole life

on fire. Because we have forgotten
the ending, the boy with green hair falls
out of frame, and we will never recall
if in our last sight of him the hair

remains—accidental, defiant—
or if he smiles bald as an internee,
or if townsfolk finally end their pursuit
after God, in a rare gesture,

tells them how to live. There are only
so many ways a murder can dissolve.
Local bullies trip over themselves
as angels, the world over, catch us

in their arms. We like that kind of story.
We've heard it before. Weightlessness. Light.

OTHER AMERICAS «««« 2010

And so he begins in the desert right in front of him,
Mexico that way, the holy mountain this way, north.

Maybe he washed up on the beach in Santa Monica
because his mother left that house. She was busy being born.

Then the man drew his profile on Montana granite. Nine hundred years,
the same gray eye on salmon, one eye inside earth.

He drifts the entire river to its mouth, down murdering chutes,
fish ladders, dodging barges on his way to William Clark.

Where the lines cross, country draining into itself, the X
above Winnemucca, the bark where Basque shepherds carve their story.

BLACK ROCK CANYON

—*at the site of Hoover Dam*

The day he nearly fell there,
concrete glared, tunnels rumbled
below, the half-mile jets made
their failed X mid-air, tumbling

at their far ends to river.
And he never thought evil
could reach through noise for ankle
or mind until then, the pull

from ledge a muscle twitch, dare
turned double-dare leaning in
to wide, grinning space. The rail
hummed in that heat. People ran

miles away along the brow
of the dam. He knew those hawks
could pick him up and have him
if they wanted. Cars drove back

and forth across the dam, riding
the idle wave that won't break
in their lifetime. Beyond them,
small boats, unbreakable blue.

THE NEXT

—*northern Nevada*

He parked in the narrow valley
beyond Wild Horse as if pulling
past the last sage, around the last moon rock
to a curb. He walked fast

into the big middle of things,
before he turned back, remembering
to unlock his car, then entered again
the edge of a center

advancing as he advanced, lines
being drawn even as he hiked,
lines he would study like the radii
of return. Who but he

or the bug-eating ascetics
would ever come to this blank place
to find the moving mouth of God, the X
on the sand repeating

as he walks toward the next, the next,
infinite as the keyboard X
he followed one day at work, far
from here, on some black map.

AUNT VIOLA HEARS PEACOCKS

They wake the neighborhood at 5:00,
crying something like a rooster
or an ape from eucalypti,
from lawns where cats will not stalk them,
from roofs, where they balance on peaks
looking sideways while tail feathers,
artful, askew, lie in casual
train down the shingles. Half a mile
west, the ponies make their wide turns
at Santa Anita. At 1:00
the announcer's call floats this far
through haze, all the smog stacking up
on her little house as cheers rise
and die with each race. She could go
inside. She could bury herself
with Manhattans and nostalgia.
Still she'd hear the scratching as they
strutted and jumped to her chimney.
In her back yard, by her pink pool,
she closes her lids and lies back
on the chaise. She winces when one
screams, but then she knows it has just
come her way in a slow, quiet
waltz to the gutter. He opens
his fan for her, curved at each end
like a shell, and it's an ocean
calling, and more eyes than she can count.

Ike golfed his last round as president
months before, uranium and krill
were discovered in Antarctica,
and Irene and Earl met at the King's X
off La Cienega, her day shift
at Douglas tucked away with letters
to the Department of Defense, the failed
renderings of bombers. They would have strolled
long at Venice Beach, skated the boardwalk.
She would have thought of them, then put the thought
away when that new man took her wrist
and whipped her forward, like the crucial
moment on *Roller Derby*, the show
she almost skated for ten years before,
lanky and quick—then pregnant with her first.

It was dark on the sand except for
the stray glow of street lamps. Irene and Earl
looked west, black as the night swam west,
and they smoked and necked. They got married
in Tijuana the Saturday
they found out about his sister. They told
everyone else the next day: Louise glad
for a father again, Pat smiling,
always, at love. Then come the days or weeks
he doesn't remember, when they never
left after all, grandparents steady
in his mind, Irene alone a lot
downstairs or late home from work. They must
have neared Valentine's Day—Alan Shepard

three months from space, Marilyn Monroe
taking her first nude swim in the White House pool—
the night he rode with Pop to drop off
Earl in Canoga Park. Long palm
boulevards cut through orange groves scenting
the night. The corner they left him at,
his house forever a blank, he wonders
why he went along. He didn't say goodbye.

The actor Jack Elam still reminds him
of Earl's face: that wide smile, those eyes glassy
with drink and enthusiasm. Earl
turned around in exotic, citrus-smelling
dark, February, 1961—
walked back to his ex- who never,
after all, was ex-. Pop and he drove home
the long way, not talking, windows
open to each neighborhood, its barking
dog, its bike in the drive, each neighborhood
a heart, the streets where homes were dark enough
for stars. Down thick, bright boulevards,
they drove home, where certainly, before
they returned, the female ritual
had already begun and ended.

CALLE REAL

At the dump behind the hill in back of
Real Street, he shot bottle, snake, and sparrow
with equal joy. He peed on the Frigidaire,
aimed rocks at a motion in debris
or love-stained bedding. He never put fire
to anything, like friends might, just to watch
curl and acceleration take their life
toward some decisive brink before
they ran. He spent those last half hours before dinner
rummaging through cold come up from the coast,

and it was not necessarily Heaven
in that new dark, and it was nothing like
Torment going home to plain cooking and six
others saying grace in unison, warm
in electric heat and the TV on
until bedtime. On the other side
of Real Street, he lingered because the bats
came out and crickets went quiet. Beyond
the hill, past his home, the reddest
western sky was sinking behind Catalina

into the sea. And the whole world could be
watching it, that slow burn through smog, an eyelash
of white that might be missile or jet
lit above the curve of earth. In his
small bowl of dusk, he emptied the rifle,
pocketed the shells for later. By now
he was thinking of where his feet landed,
the last twitches of a bird, the puma
just now leaving her cave somewhere close. Then
these lamps, all these houses that knew him.

MIGRATION

No one talked about the whales till our teens,
endangered all century, out of sight
on wide, long detours around human beings.
Then newspapers filled with their greasy line

north to south, so close to the coast we could
see them from our benches, find them in small
boats where the creatures nudged our hulls and sprayed.

What else didn't we know? We saw that hook
the shark made in a fin. We saw the tail
splash us backward, sink glistening into gray.

HE WILL NEVER BE MEXICAN LIKE OSCAR QUIROZ

Those days still looking for pity, the boy
pictured himself in hospital beds, weak
with disease. Or he saw a father's hand
so often flat at his face, running away
made the only sense. He lived in a box
near imagined rights-of-way, fresh oranges
falling. He begged drivers for cash and meat.
Once his photo made the *Times*, homes unlocked
throughout the Basin, the hearts of rich strangers
moved to pull him from the dangerous street

to new life without fear. Where Oscar
came from, the boy never knew. Only that
it lay deep in Mexico, a place that scarred
the new boy's face somehow, left a rattle
in his chest, kept his family too far south
of any wealth or simple English. Now
the boys joined desks and worked on math. Oscar
still used hands, all his fingers blurring brown
and flying in place above the page. How
to tell him *Wrong* even when the numbers

fit? How could Oscar ever learn to talk?
Those days still looking for pity, the boy
went without imagined meals and cash, spoke
Spanish to the oaks. When every human
sound made him dizzy, every face frowning
to understand, he knew he'd finally come
to some new country, not Mexico—to some
place past confused or angry hands. The whole town
gathered there, smiling fluently, pointing
here and *here* at every American thing.

The girl from the next block told him Baptists
ruled because *We don't have to do this,*
she said, and danced her hands across her chest,
meaning the sign of the cross, and someone
called her *Okie,* which explained a lot
later, when aerospace went flat and her
father moved. There are Americas
you never dream of. Oscar Quiroz sat
next to him his first months in California.
The boy could hardly say his name, shy as dirt
and with no common language. By the end
of the year, when Judy Lopez died, when
Mrs. LaLonde assigned Oscar to be
pall bearer, he knew enough to say *Never*
and fainted to the Mission brick. It was
another world two years before in the gray
TV where the assassin was shot
in his white shirt and a horse drew the caisson
past federal granite. We were different
people, new chapters of ourselves, by the time
we walked that same street with our kids. We opened
to its color like books.

              And in the desert,
those towns like Boron, Tonopah, or Wells,
what did people do afternoons it wasn't
too hot? He saw them walking in pairs past
ocotillo and yucca toward the lowest
spot in the valley, the place the lake forms
those few weeks each winter, then evaporates.

In Montana, he knew a white man who
lived three years in a tipi inviting
Wakantanka to join him. And Andy
jumped out the 27th floor window
on West 72nd. And Patty moved back
and forth from Provincetown to Key West, looking
for her father. Chicago burned again,
thanks to Daley's thugs. And here, frozen
in Minnesota, 100 miles up
a tributary of the Upper Mississippi,
current pulls hard as summer toward the Gulf.
On the gallows, 1862,
the Indians sang the only hymn
in their own language, not a death chant
as reported. Thirty-eight Dakota
sang to the same god as spectators,
and it was the day after Christmas at
the river's edge, the snap of their necks
pulled toward the Gulf. There are countries
you never dream of.

       In 1962,
he floated on his back in Lake Mead.
The petroglyphs could not look out at him
from their deep dark, and he could not hear them
from our boat, riding a hundred feet
of water, winding through the quiet
narrows, the drowned gorge. We glided beside
the Arizona border, through layers of
ever-younger stone. We trolled over
the footpaths of ghosts,
each scuff mark and splinter

Powell left passing through time. Even when
he stands in one place, there is another
country waiting for him to discover it,
under the skin of water, under blistering
sky. There is another America beyond
his naïve, disappearing skin.

                          Walt Whitman,
it has come time to praise and curse the reach
of your arms across minor hills and through
barren cities, where the beautiful, godly,
even the ugly and deranged, gather
under your beard. How narrow our life
by comparison, your flesh sent out in eddies,
an electric storm perforating these small
cosmos of cells. How casual your call
that we kiss the face of AIDS on the lips
and wash the feet of the beaten. In that
famous photograph where you hold
a butterfly, a fake paper prop, you
nearly bring it to life with your breath,
or so we would believe. Walt Whitman,
you have ruined the earth for us, praising
oily lagoon and salt palace alike,
drag queen and heiress, starling and finch, all
because you will observe no difference
that ever mattered to God. You take in
every bit of continent and breathe
it out again. Bridge, lizard, virus,
ambulance, tornado, gold ring, false teeth,
apple orchard, factory, revolver,
gangrenous foot, opera, gallows trap door,
president, guitar, encyclopedia—

Even as you lie under snow and brown
lawns where you make your claim, we will not
find you as we look for you, we will not
hear you as we listen, we will not answer
as you ask too much. Still, you might touch us
anyway, a wind from two directions,
little girl wondering out loud where grass
has gone, your finger on the national grief.

TO DICK OF THE STORMS

Sometimes we dream the heroic canvas
where you charge Seattle to St. Regis,
naming every interior gull, where
the army of you moves up the Clark Fork,
steady on stone and fishtail, easy
with wind, those black clouds at your back, to where
town finally begins, the homes absorbing
all their blank doors until you find us.

We knew how you failed your own body. Like
ours, your greatest moments were imagined
beyond their wildest potential. We knew
that sword, honed mornings at a round kitchen
table, dulled in afternoon fields. We forgave
all that, loved that you were more like us than us.

A LAKE IN NORTHWEST MONTANA

Hard to know what drove him that far,
L.A. ablaze one day, his car
lurching through the mountain pass
and into desert. We wondered
if the Feds pursued him, or thugs
he could never name. How fast

would anyone know he cut east
at Bishop, creeks in their steady
decline, the creosote burned
out of leaning fence posts? Would they
know he bet a wad of twenties
every town from Tonopah

to Jackpot? That Twin Falls
found him boozy by daybreak, all
the big money gone, all these
robed men leaning out each front door
to get the morning news? And where
did the next life start, with eggs

at the Jordan Café, the roads
thin, still a day's drive past Arco?
Over the pass to the next
state, who would have guessed that far north—
a lake filling the view, the larch
thickening around its edges—

who would have guessed him still a goner
trolling for salmon at the terse

middle of things? Four miles out
in river drift, he drew the wide
circle above fish, dodging weed
and bare logs, drew the target

for some dark plane or avenging
angel. Still, he made the move
to do himself in, one turn
at a time, while salmon wavered
below, and the bull trout farther
down, where the last light had gone.

FUR-BEARING TROUT

He liked the mornings that would stay still
and end up hot, there in the middle
drift of Flathead Lake, trolling a vast melt
three hundred feet deep, days ago spilled

out of Glacier Park. If salmon rose
in such weather, it was to follow
cutthroat and light to the gnat-hatch above.
If salmon dove, it was to follow

cold into the room of mackinaw
and Dolly Varden, a place of raw
harm where the school would scatter before char
as if a gun had fired. In flat calm

on the surface, his skin burned, he let
yards of line out every ten minutes.
He reeled in part every five, the mountains
huge in each direction, like still fish,

like fur-bearing trout on those postcards
tourists loved. His small boat hummed forward.
Then rifle shots across the mouth of sky,
hooks coming at him from every shore.

FAMOUS DANCING BEARS

In a memory he no longer
trusts, the great Russian beast turns figure-eights
on ice, its glinting skates quivering under
the weight. People in the oval dark say

Oh! or whistle at the thin peasant girl
imprisoned in leotard, joined by pinkie
to a bear. The couple segues to an awkward
waltz, the music bright, the animal taking lead,

and he remembers Yogi and Boo-Boo
gliding cheek-to-cheek through Jellystone Park.
The hunter lurks, and smokes, and lets fly sparks
Smokey has to douse to keep in step with who

he is. Despite chains or harm, they choose to *be*,
in woods, on tour—or by the hearth, like Roethke.

RAIN

1.

He could never tell you with what mixture
of grief his mother dished out each *No*. Nor
if he ever heard her praise him to friends.
He always breathed deeply in Los Angeles,
riding his bike along the thin sidewalk
above the Basin. Only City Hall
punched through smog. Only his feet and eyes

took him anywhere good, and one long day
he pedaled toward the tar pits until he
convinced himself he was lost, the dark faces
kind enough but the streets too flat to know.
In Santa Monica, the roller coaster
looped, curved, and banked figure-eights at the end
of a shaky pier. He can't remember

if fire or a Mexican storm took it.
He does know fuchsias burn when Santa Ana
wind sucks heat out of the desert. Chinese
elms do not root deep enough for some long
rains. At Holy Cross Cemetery, his
great-grandparents lay next to Rita Hayworth,
Charles Boyer, Rosalind Russell, Ray Bolger,

Bela Lugosi, Louella Parsons,
Jimmy Durante, Spike Jones, Bing Crosby,
Sharon Tate, and Gloria Vanderbilt.
His grandfather bought two bouquets

each time they visited, arranging flowers
in sunken cups, polishing the flat stones
with green wax paper. Who would have guessed

C.C. Brown's, 100 years selling hot fudge,
could ever close? He could never tell you
how much pleasure it was summer nights
to drive under burning hills to Hollywood
for ice cream. Or to find snow on the patio
one morning each decade. How could you know
what living without a father meant to him,

missing hand on the back, across the face,
missing animal in the house,
the bonus of mercy where a mother,
failing, is taken in by her parents
to make a new kind of family? He didn't
know, wouldn't have wanted, anything
different. They belonged on that cul-de-sac

with the house no one entered or left,
with the house of seven children, the house
of suing neighbors, in the neighborhood
of midnight calls those weeks his family
showed the house to Blacks. He could try to say
what it meant to move south to the small town,
the ocean in sight, but that would put him

ahead of himself. There's no leaving behind
Aunt Viola's peacocks in Arcadia,
the giant donut on the way to LAX,
the Dodge up the street opening a backyard

wall, and everyone pulling newspapers
from spaces inside the brick. He saw the
Graf Zeppelin land in Long Beach, read of

Chamberlain denounced, four orphans rescued
by a has-been actor with a big house
and dog. If he drew the map where Slauson
and La Brea crossed at the heart, and
Springhill Place an inch off-center, hovering
up its steep steps from the parking lot
for Thrifty and Fox, if he inked in

hydrangea, green stucco, the rare pervert
lurking near the edge in rhododendra,
all pets held fast to their properties, then
the picture might go symbolic, aerial,
and no one could see inside the garage
where Chester, from down the hill, showed Corrine
his dick and scared her to tears. No one could

hear murmuring ancients next door propped
on their narrow stoop and waiting for a bike
or car to circle back at their round end
of street. Better not to pretend paper,
or even an atlas of paper, fixes
anything for more than a moment. He
moved south. His mother died thirty-one years

later in another city. The record
shows she left Los Angeles with a newborn
daughter. It's always dangerous to explain,
but he thinks he knows the heartache

of those last two years in L.A., no husband
in sight, and eight years divorced, and Catholic,
and all in brilliant 1962.

The Baldwin Dam had not yet cracked. Watts had not
burned. Even now, he couldn't know the hurt
a great-aunt caused at Easter table, or eyes
at the communion rail, a white host pausing
in midair. It's always dangerous
to explain, but he tries over and over:
declaring the Union honest, that he's seen

the wooden road that used to lead to Las Vegas,
and the house, not far from the studios,
where Wyatt Earp died of kidney failure
in 1929. What more could make
a place live again, or convince you it
was important? He could draw the wash of air,
the back of an Impala convertible

aiming toward Manhattan Beach, sunburn, kelp.
Or the ride he and his grandfather
gave Earl Huntoon—the brief, illegal
step-father—back to Canoga Park, back
one hot night down wide boulevards, the palms
high and dark and unrelenting block
after block, back to the first wife who never

really left. Or the weight of a storm grate
on his thumb. Or the oleander cave
behind his house. Fern. Snail. The banned
incinerator. Or the episode,

twenty years after moving, where he finds
Earl, his youngest sister's dad, in credits
for a TV western. Never a word,

and there the phantom was, a property
master for *How the West Was Won*.
Take away anger, and you still have race.
Take away rage, and you still have shame.
His mother lay down at night, a city
glittering behind her door, breaking the laws.
The city spread out at night, a mother

full of last breaths waiting for the rare
tropical storm or the absolute calm
before an earthquake. She belongs to the
avenues, the missing trolleys, Ben Hur's
chariot under glass at the Pacific
Pantages Theater, April 1959.
She is the movie he can't film or

explain, the city he can't find without
forgiveness. And just out of reach, the heart
of town prepares to riot and burn
while the greater body, lush with gardens
quenched on their stolen water, settles in
for the evening on a glistening bed,
and pulls down ash from the air like rain.

2.

Look, I'll be honest. He believes believing
crucial. He wants you to know this all really
happened to him: fatherless in utero,
born to woman both damaged human being
and burned, breathing landscape. What would it mean,
he wonders, if you knew driving Angeles Crest
the only way left to love her? You might

change your life. Might look for the darkest road
in town to find a mouth, the oracle
leading you back to a bright kitchen, one
camelia afloat in the jelly jar
on the round table, someone whistling, as much
in the sensate world as you'll ever be.
You might believe him to believe the world.

3.

As for me, I don't really care. I invent
rose beds as easily as I remember them.
I had a father once, too, left behind
for the crime of spending paychecks, one month
to the next, in Mexico. I won't
allow you the privilege of sympathy.
I will not play victim or hero, will not

redeem those weeks you relished cruelty,
slurring the waiter in front of client
or friend. You'll have to take care of your own

child inside, its constant whine for all things
unnatural, for the whole world's pity.
What I'll give you in return is an ordinary
object made from air you breathed once yourself,

fire you almost died in. Let's carry it
together to Los Angeles or Pittsburgh,
flame in the hand that never burns the hand.
Let's find the Los Angeles hill, the New
Orleans churchyard where we're buried among
celebrities, standing on top of ourselves
as each new pulse invents the next. Now is when

you arrange the memorial for all
time. You lay down the sprays on etched granite.
You lie down beside your eternal flame.
Or you don't: You walk across grass to a
gate opening to a street filled with oaks, near
dead from wilt. Each animal, each person
you meet stirs a little before the rain.

Meanwhile, the hero moves south,

4.

                              his mother
dies thirty-one years later in another
city. By then the Chaco petroglyphs
glow and fade on her skin. The open pits
at Butte and Ely track the cancer's path
inside her nose. The Colorado blue
to brown in her veins, the Coos Bay bridge guides

steelhead to her tired side. Everywhere West
takes a feature for its own, and if the barest
desert floor chooses that square inch of skin
over hip bone, then Flathead Lake assumes
her eye, and all minor rivers her hair
and tendons, Portland her mind, Los Angeles
the heart that finally will not beat. The Rockies

burn into the fall with August lightning,
and cattle are streaming out of high forests
into her arms. But she's too old to care
for everything. The body, organ by
organ, disconnects beneath the surface
as if a nuclear test rearranged
the interior of earth. He barely knows

anymore what fish did her laughing, what
kind of siskins sent her last messages
to God. He moves field to town, everywhere
learning a new landscape without her,
the new words only he can say. From farther
away than he can see, the clouds are coming.
Already the ashes are making plans.

NOTES

NEW POEMS

"'Northumbrian Miner at His Evening Meal'": This poem and all of the poems based on classic photographs take their occasions from *The Art of Photography 1839-1989* (Yale University Press).

"Trace" is in memory of John Cuchessi.

THE UNTESTED HAND

"Evening News" is after a poem of the same title by William Stafford.

RADIOACTIVE CITY

"Scene from a 1948 Movie" refers to *The Boy with Green Hair,* directed by Joseph Losey.

OTHER AMERICAS

"To Dick of the Storms" is in memory of Richard Hugo.

"A Lake in Northwest Montana" is in memory of Robert Annand.

ACKNOWLEDGMENTS

NEW POEMS

Some of the new poems in this book appeared first, sometimes in different form, in the following publications. Many thanks to their editors:

JOURNALS

Bennington Review: "In Milosz's Room"
Borderlands: Texas Poetry Review: "Northumbrian Miner at His Evening Meal"
Cincinnati Review: "Impossible Dream"
Field: "God Particles," "Old Country Portraits"
Four Corners: "The truth is"
The Georgia Review: "Recovery"
Green Mountains Review: "Violence"
Harvard Review: "Pacific Crest"
Hotel Amerika: "The House"
Laurel Review: "The End of a Long Winter North in the Northern Hemisphere,"
    "Floyd and Lucille Burroughs, Hale County, Alabama"
Miramar: "Going-to-the-Sun Highway," "In Milosz's Bed"
New Walk: "Impossible Modesty," "Impossible Wilderness"
Permafrost: "A Map of the World"
Poet Lore: "The Reading Light"
Poetry Northwest: "How to Read a Poem," "The Martian Poet," "The Women of Lockerbie"
Profane: "History"
A Public Space: "When the Other Man Asked Him Did He Pray"
Santa Fe Literary Review: "Cul-de-Sac"
Smartish Pace: "Near Roslin Institute, Midlothian, Scotland"
South Dakota Review: "Memoir"
Sugar House Review: "Leaving the City"
Weber: The Contemporary West: "Calculation," "Kitchen," "Trace," "Turpentine"

ANTHOLOGIES

The Blueroad Reader: Stardust and Fate: "Never"
Confusion of Stars: "The End of a Long Winter North in the Northern Hemisphere,"
    "Floyd and Lucille Burroughs, Hale County, Alabama," "Near Roslin Institute,
    Midlothian, Scotland"
Minnesota English Journal Online: "Recovery"
The 99th Annual Awards Ceremony: Award-Winning Poems: "Aphasiac"
On the Wing: American Poems of Air and Space Flight: "The Women of Lockerbie"
Where One Voice Ends Another Begins: 150 Years Of Minnesota Poetry: "Near Roslin Institute,
    Midlothian, Scotland"

For help with *Body Turn to Rain*, I'm grateful to the following writers:

Thomas Aslin, David Axelrod, Ralph Burns, Brian Frink, Thomas Mitchell, Sarah Snook, and Samantha Ten Eyck for their readings, their comments, and their own fine work.

Early believers Jorge Evans, Robert Hedin, Melissa Kwasny, Matt Mauch, Edward Micus, Jim Peterson, Lee Ann Roripaugh, William Trowbridge.

Reality-checkers Art Homer, Liz Kay, Gordon Preston.

2007 spring workshop students David Clisbee, Jenny Yang Cropp, Luke Daly, Britt Steiger Frank, Jon Surdo, Darren Wieland, for our self-designed forms.

2012 Hawthornden Castle fellows Ben Clark, Victoria Field, Sarah Howe, Hamish Robinson, Rebecca Swift, and Rory Waterman. We worked hard. We made a nice group.

The ever-believing Candace Black. The uncountable hearts.

Thanks to the following organizations for fellowships, awards, or the gift of space that helped make possible some of the work included in this collection:

The Centrum Foundation
Hawthornden International Retreat for Writers
The Loft Literary Center
The McKnight Foundation
The Minnesota State Arts Board
Minnesota State University Mankato Faculty Research, Teaching Scholar, and Summer
    Research programs
The National Endowment for the Arts
Poetry Society of America
Prairie Lakes Regional Arts Council

"Richard Robbins is a fiscal year 2016 recipient of an Artist Initiative grant from the Minnesota State Arts Board. This activity is made possible by the voters of Minnesota through a grant from the Minnesota State Arts Board, thanks to a legislative appropriation by the Minnesota State Legislature; and by a grant from the National Endowment for the Arts."

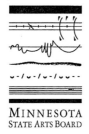

MINNESOTA
STATE ARTS BOARD

ART WORKS.

National
Endowment
for the Arts
arts.gov